BIBLE
LESSONS
FROM OUR
PETS

Volume 1

DAVID SMITH

BIBLE LESSONS FROM OUR PETS
Copyright © 2011 by David Smith

PCG Legacy, a division of Pilot Communciations Group, Inc.
317 Appaloosa Trail Waco, TX 76712

ISBN: 978-1-936417-25-4

Printed in the United States of America

www.biblelessonsfromourpets.com

Dedication & Introduction

Anytime I speak to people about my book, they often respond by saying, "Wow, that is a great idea!" or "How did you get that idea?" Well, I can't take total credit because the seed was planted deep into my heart by the Lord with a love for all animals. He gave me the ability to see what was happening in the recesses of my heart by using His majestic creation. And over the course of the last few years, He has been speaking to me by using my cat, Bling. I wish I could say that I always listened, but sadly, no. The lessons were always there and God freely gave me the option to listen to the daily lessons He provided.

Obeying or not, I always have had my cat to entertain and teach me. To me, Bling is an amazing creature filled to the brim with her own special personality. She is, first and foremost, my cat. Even though my wife, Buffy, rescued her, she has become my girl. I will often find her sleeping between my legs, or on me, or just in my general vicinity. With a house full of two cats and a persistent pup, she has ruled the roost by laying the beat down on any other animal that gets in her way. She is determined and she is powerful, not just in her catlike physique, but in her personality. She has fully stepped into her catness and no one or nothing will change that. I do admire how she always seems to be comfortable in her own skin, I mean fur, and that she isn't afraid of anyone. Bling is who she is, and she knows it. She has overcome her own giants and

survived. It seems silly to see so much in a cat, but I sure know that I would like to step fully into how God has made me and not be afraid of anybody or anything and knowing full well my strengths and weaknesses. This is the animal that God used to show me Him. And He still uses this feline to this very day.

God is the only reason I have endured with the idea of making pet lessons into a book. Normally, fear would have overtaken me long ago, but the Lord has place people and teachings before me to use as a weapon against the debilitating disease of fear. I am not a professional writer, nor do I claim any special accomplishment, but just because I am not and have not, does not mean that I cannot do so. All God did was place a desire in my heart and, unlike the many other great ideas that came before me, I conquered the giant of fear. Therefore, I encourage you to step into whom God has made you—not what others think or say about you. Sometimes you will have to not listen to what your own mind tells you for our "hearts are deceitful above all things and beyond cure. Who can understand it?" Don't let the enemy talk you out of your deepest desires of your heart. God placed them there and the only ones we have to blame for not following through with them is ourselves. Take today to choose you and God, not the world.

I take great inspiration from my wife, Buffy. She has always been supportive and there for me when times got tough. She helped me stay on course in the good times and the bad and I have taken great joy in all of her. God seems to have put a powerful and strong woman in my life, because Buffy, along with Bling, is all of that. She is an amazingly determined girl who does not take no for an answer and will not back down from a challenge. What an amazing woman and friend God has given me to walk through this life! Thank you, my bride!

CONTENTS

Foreword

We can learn much about a person by listening to their words, spoken or written. The book you hold in your hands should not just be read but be listened to. Listen to the textured perspectives David relates in his unique experiences. Listen to how he draws out meaning, encouragement and even comfort from the lessons formed from these encounters. Listen as he weaves together insights about God, faith and life from each character he introduces us too.

Listen to a man who is introducing us to his world. A world where his values were formed and passed along. A world where his caring connects with our hearts, and his openness and authenticity becomes alluring and captivating. This is David's world and you are welcome here.

I've known David Smith for many years now. First, as his Pastor, then as his boss and finally as his friend. I've listened to him expound on faith, football, church life, special projects, varieties of people, and last but not least his dreams for his future. In this, I've heard more than his words—I've heard his heart. I've seen his work. I've watched him grow. His dreams are beginning to bud and bloom and you are holding one of these in your hands right now.

Find a place to curl up and relax. Grab a cup of something warm and keep it close. To this recipe for relaxation, add David's book and you have all the ingredients needed for hours of enjoyment. Remember, listen, you will be surprised and delighted at what David (and God) will say to you today. Enjoy!

Jon Oletzke
Pastor, Stone Church
Yakima, Washington

Facing the Fire

by David Smith

I think our cat has a love affair with a portable heater. It may sound crazy, but it's completely true. Almost any chance she gets, she's face first in front of the heater, "catching some sun," as Buffy and I like to call it. She even lies in front of the heater in anticipation of it being turned on. Our Bling is obsessed!

One day, she got a little too close to her best friend and the whiskers on the right side of her face were singed badly. I would have thought she would have given the heater a rest after leaving the right side of her face smoldering; however, she returned to her love, regardless of the dangers. "Isn't this just like me," I thought, "after getting too close to sin and getting burned, I go back for more pain."

I don't think it's just me that has walked on the hot coals of sin only to turn around and walk on that fiery path again, but I'm sure everyone has been there and wears the t-shirt.

Proverbs 26:11 describes this perfectly:

"As a dog returns to its vomit,
so a fool repeats his foolishness."

Now, I don't know about you, but going back to eating my puke is not too appetizing. Vomit has nasty chunks in it, smells, and, well, that pretty much describes it, but sin generally has the same appearance, but only to the trained eye.

When I lie, it's to protect myself in the moment from an argument or being hurt, but what I'm not always seeing is the damage it's doing to my heart and to my relationship with the Lord. When I go back to sin, whatever that sin is, it leaves a nasty vomit aftertaste in my heart and this aftertaste becomes a barrier between me and the Lord.

God wants to be close to his children, but if the smell of vomit is emanating from our heart, then He may not want to come too close. As believers, we ought to keep our hearts cleaned up so that we are ready to be in the Lord's presence. Jesus said in Matthew 5:8,

"Blessed are the pure in heart
for they shall see God."

So, let's watch what we see, say, and do because God is just waiting to have a deeper relationship with us!

Blind Date

by Chloe Young

When I was 16, I decided to try my hand at dog-breeding. I studied and researched, acquired a lovely black toy poodle named Ashley, chose a little Yorkie stud named Tommy, and then I studied and researched some more. I so wanted to do everything just right.

Nine weeks after her 'blind date' with Tommy, my poodle had four wonderful little puppies. Three males and one female; all of them pure black like their mamma. In no time at all, I knew each of them like the back of my own hand. There was the little one we called Spitfire. There was the loner—always off by himself, doing his own thing. The female was AKA as The Boss. And the calm-but-playful one we called Patches (due to an unfortunate haircut adventure.)

I watched them day and night, 24/7. It was like they were my own babies. Each one was identical to the others at a stranger's first glance, but to me each was so unique and individual. Every one was precious in its own way.

My careful studying and research wasn't wasted. I made sure that everything was done in the right way, at the right time--except for the weaning. Ashley decided she'd rather be my baby than their mamma. I had to force her to stay with them so they could eat, but even at that, she began to dry up early and they weren't getting enough. I decided that it would be best to start weaning them a bit early to compensate for the lack of milk.

I remember the first time I tried to feed a bit of warm, watered-down, hamburger to the first puppy. His cute little teddy-bear face wrinkled up and he pulled his head back as far as it would go, determined to keep this new, foreign substance out of his mouth. It was so cute; I could hardly focus through my own laughter.

But I persisted, knowing that there's not a dog on earth that doesn't LOVE raw meat and that this was the best way to get food into his belly. I finally managed to get a tiny bit into his mouth; before I knew it, he was chewing on my, now very clean, finger, determined to find more of this amazing substance.

Proverbs 3:5 says,

> *"Trust in the Lord with all your*
> *heart and lean not on your*
> *own understanding."*

I so often find myself behaving just like that little puppy when I encounter something new. I close my mouth and pull back, rejecting it. I don't want to try something new; I'm comfortable with what I'm accustomed to.

But God knows best, doesn't He? He wants me to have what is better than that with which I am familiar. He knows that, in the long run, not only will it be better, but I will like it better, too. In fact, I'll LOVE IT. This is all because He wants me to be happy, to have better and to be better--always more and better.

Do I have to accept what he offers me? No. Will He force me? Never. The choice is always mine. But God ALWAYS knows best. I'm still learning to trust in him even when I'm afraid of something new, even when I don't like the looks of it.

All I have to do is 'taste' it. Just like my puppy.

My Stupid Cat!

by Sabrina Young

As I was growing up, we always had animals. We had cats, dogs, lizards, hamsters and even rats. Of all the animals we kept around our house, there was one that always stood out to me. He was very special, not a typical cat, and let's just say he had some character!

I remember the day my dad came home with our cat (which was a kitten when we got him). He was a grey tabby with black stripes and had ears that were way too large for his face — it was love at first sight for my mother and us kids! My dad, however, took a little longer to fall in love with this adorable little kitten.

Although cute (no one could deny that), he was a bit noisy during the night hours. He liked to play at night, so my dad set up a "play area" in our dining room that was completely secure of him getting free to roam the house. However, this plan back-fired. Instead of getting woke up from a kitten playing with your toes, you were awakened by a high-pitched, screechy "MEOW!" that would continue through the entire night.

My dad would yell from his room, "Be quiet, you stupid cat!" And, that is how our cat got his name, Stupid. Cruel?

Maybe. But as the years went on, our family all grew to love Stupid with everything we had. He became part of our family.

Stupid was a cat that had character — all of the dogs on the block trembled when he came outside. He was dominant, fearless, and secure in his "cathood." Yet, despite this dominance, Stupid was uniquely sensitive to our family. He was loving, obedient, and missed us when we were away from home.

On one particular occasion, Stupid was the only comfort I had. My childhood was a difficult one — I lost my mother, gained a new mother, lost a friend to suicide, and lost my grandmother all within a span of a few years. My grandmother was arguably the most difficult loss for me, because of all the previous losses, it felt like the last straw. I was almost 12 at the time.

I remember feeling that God was a million miles away; I wondered how He could possibly care about me with all of the negative things happening in my life. Maybe He was just too busy? I couldn't comprehend this God and I desperately needed to know He cared. When I heard the news of my grandmother's passing, I sat on my stairs and wept. I was angry, upset, sad, grief-stricken, and I felt completely abandoned.

Just as I was trying to sort my thoughts, Stupid came walking by. I looked up at him and he stopped walking. We had a moment where we just stared at each other. This may sound strange, but I could see the concern in his eyes as we just sat there and stared at one another. Stupid then slowly walked towards me, stopped in front of me, looked at me again, then laid on my feet.

He laid there with me while I wept for what seemed like an hour (I don't know the exact span of time). At that moment, I knew he was sent from God. I still did not understand this God, but I knew that he cared enough to gift me with a cat that demonstrated the Lord's mercy and love.

Later, I read the scripture in Psalm 34:17-18 which reads,

> *"The righteous cry out, and the Lord hears them;*
> *He delivers them from all their troubles.*
> *The Lord is close to the brokenhearted and*
> *saves those who are crushed in spirit."*

To this day, whenever I hear that verse, I thank God for the "stupid" cat that was adopted into our family at just the right time in my life.

Bailey's Love

by Steve and Catherine Platt

What can I say about Bailey. She is an 8-pound Chi-Pin with the most gentle and loving manner you could ever ask for. Bailey loves to hug and snuggle. When you pick her up, she immediately snuggles and "melts" right in to you. It's so nice after a long hard day to know I can come home and receive unconditional love from someone that won't judge my actions, ask for anything, or talk back.

Bailey came into our life 7 years ago at 12-weeks old and weighing in at 1.8 pounds. She is not a typical small dog; she's not nervous, doesn't bark constantly, isn't grouchy or snappy, and doesn't make messes anywhere. Bailey loves everyone, she has never met a stranger. She greets everyone she meets with a snuggle and the softest licks of her big toungue. Yes, she has her favorite people, but she offers her friendship to anyone who will accept it.

Given her gentle spirit, we decided to let her have a litter of puppies. WOW what a wonderful mother Bailey turned out to be. Bailey's first litter was three little girls who were as fat as they could be. It seemed that from the time they were born, Bailey went into overdrive licking, cleaning, feeding, and snuggling — yes snuggling. Bailey's puppies had her full attention even when they were sleeping. She seemed to smile as she just lay and snuggled with them.

When Bailey's puppies were about 4 weeks old, she had a day where she seemed agitated and nervous, she was just unable to settle down. But as typical, Bailey was as attentive to the puppies as she always was.

Evening came and she began shaking and her legs collapsed out from under her. I called the vet, rushed her in and she was put on an I.V. overnight. I became a puppy surrogate; feeding them every two hours. I tried to put them back in their bed, but because they were used to their mamas snuggles, they whined until I brought them in to bed with me.

Bailey was able to come home the next day with a diagnosis of eclampsia. She was such a good mother that she gave all of her own stored calcium supply to her puppies, even though it would almost cost her life.

One of our greatest needs as human beings is to be loved. We need to know that we are important to somebody, that somebody truly cares about us, wants us, and accepts us unconditionally. Bailey's love for her puppies was a clear example of great love.

How much greater is God's love for us?

God's love is self-giving, God's love is sacrificial, God's love is unconditional. There is not one good thing in any of us that merits God's love.

As Jesus laid down his life for his Love of us, Bailey was willing to give her life for her puppies.

John 15:9-16 says,

"As the Father has loved me, so have I loved you.

Abide in my love. . . . Greater love
has no one than this; that someone lay down
his life for his friends."

Romans 5:6-8 says,

"Very rarely will anyone die for
a righteous man, though for a good man
someone might possibly die. But God
demonstrates His own love for us in this:
while we were still sinners,
Christ died for us."

The Montana Man

by Larry & Helen Mast

Born and raised in Montana, I feel somewhat qualified to write about what I call the "Montana Man." I think we have a highly developed sense of independence, a pioneer spirit—"I can go it alone." It's nice to have other people around, but I can handle things myself, thank you. Why should I bleed all over everybody? I could say we are a breed apart, but that's probably not true. I have found similar men and mindsets elsewhere.

Independence is most likely a learned response, gained during childhood and beyond. I spent a lot of time alone as a boy, when I wasn't in school or milking cows. With our two farm dogs, Shep and Lad, I explored every acre and knew every square foot, tree, and fencepost on our 560-acre farm. The dogs and I kept the skunk and porcupine population under control. Alone was something I liked. It's a wonder I didn't turn into a hermit.

Then, at age twelve, I went forward one evening during a revival service at Mountain View Mennonite Church and accepted God's free gift of salvation. That remains the single most important decision I ever made in my life.

In the following years, I began to change by opening up to people and sharing my needs and feelings. Openness is a must for a good marriage. I still withdraw on occasion, but I've come a long way since those skunk-and-porcupine days.

During a time of stress and personal introspection, in regards to my battle with prostate cancer, I wrote the following letter and request for prayer. It was a cry from my heart, sent out mostly by email to many of our friends. Never in my wildest dreams did I imagine it would generate the response it did. Phone calls, cards, and emails flooded in from friends in nineteen different countries.

Hope is Faith on Tiptoes

I had my regular physical exam in January and the doctor discovered elevated PSA numbers, plus an irregularity on my prostate. The doctor said I could keep my previous short-term work commitment onboard the Mercy Ship, so it was April before I had the recommended biopsy. That brought the unwelcome news that I have prostate cancer. In a consultation with the urologist today, he stressed the importance of a timely decision. He only recommends surgery, radiation, or hormone treatment. We are also considering health food supplements and diet change. Our times are in God's hands and we need to hear His words of encouragement and leading. Please pray for healing and wisdom as we make a decision.

Friday evening while sitting in our living room, I felt overwhelmed, and, quite frankly, a little discouraged. I was idly watching the birds at the feeders on our back porch. Suddenly, five Indigo Buntings appeared and began feeding. They stayed for nearly an hour. Never have we seen more than one of these beautiful birds at a time!

Jesus performed a miracle with five loaves and two fish. My two-fold part could be having faith and hope in an almighty, faithful, and loving God. Several days ago I heard someone say "Hope is faith—on tiptoes."

Over the years we have often asked our friends for prayer. Today, we come to you again, knowing our Father hears and answers when we call on Him.

Standing on Tiptoes, Larry & Helen Mast

(Today, Larry is cancer free. He had robotic surgery to remove the prostate and is doing fine.)

Chasing Bear

by Laura Schilling

In the year 1999, I was questioning how God could love a filthy sinner like me. I had done many things to disappoint myself, my family and most of all God. How could I face Him now? God answered this question in a special way, by sending me a little friend, who I called "Bear."

I first encountered Bear in the Safeway parking lot. He was a sweet, fuzzy, black little ball of fur. Someone had found him abandoned in an orchard. I immediately produced my $20 dollars and scooped up this little bundle of energy. He was my new best friend.

Bear tested my patience right from the beginning. He pooped and peed on the floor a lot. He wanted to play at 2 a.m. and would whine when I told him to go to sleep. He would drag my underwear off and chew on them. I would get so irritated and wonder why I was putting myself through all of this.

Then he would look up at me with those dark brown puppy dog eyes and place a sweet smelling, wet puppy kiss on my nose. I would forget what a pain he could be and my heart would swell with love.

As Bear grew, so did his annoying characteristics. One of his favorites was waiting until the door was ajar and then jetting out into the street. He would turn and look at me with a sparkle in his eyes. His look said, "Catch me if you can."

I would chase him all over the neighborhood. My heart pounded with fear that he would get hit by a car. I would finally give up and head home in tears, praying that he would be safe and come back home. He would eventually come back with his tongue hanging loose and out of breath. He would fall to the floor in a hurry and give out a satisfied sigh.

When I first had a date with my now husband Jason, Bear sat on the floor next to us and quietly shredded the arm of his brand new Eddie Bauer Jacket. Jason got up to leave and put his arm in the gooey gnarled arm of his nice corduroy jacket. Needless to say, their future relationship was strained.

We would often take Bear up in the mountains for hikes. Bear did not like cars. He would hang his head over our shoulders and make a high pitched whining sound followed by loud panting. He was relentless the whole way there and back. My husband and I would both look at him and say, "shush Bear!" Nothing would stop him. We tried Benadryl, Valarian drops and more Benadryl. Jason would say, "I don't know why you love that crazy dog so much!"

You see, Bear taught me a bit of how God must feel about us. He loves us in spite of our annoying, sometimes dangerous habits.

We run from Him and He chases after us. He is worried about what happens to us when we stray from Him. God just wants to be with us, because we are his children. I am convinced that God loves me even more than I loved Bear.

"But when the kindness and love of God
our Savior appeared, he saved us,
not because of righteous things we had done,
but because of his mercy."
— Titus 3:4-5

The Chow Dog Learns Patience

by Katherin B. FitzPatrick

Adapted from "Karen Loved a Dog Named CiCi,"
from "Angel Promises…" By K.B. FitzPatrick

She came to us back in 1993, a three-month-old bundle of lovable red fur, large expressive eyes, and a tongue that often wanted to lick our faces. Our friends across town had two red chow dogs and whenever we came over to see them our girls just loved playing with them!

Chows are known for being watch dogs with powerful jaws and very strong shoulders and forearms. Sometimes, only a one-person dog, one has to be careful how you approach them unless there is a positive nod from the master's head and voice. Doug and Donna had worked hard to "People-ize" their two Chinese Chows and visitors to their home could feel comfortable with their good natured dogs. But some instincts can still remain intact. Chows are known for hating and killing cats!

"One time, an unsuspecting cat came sailing over the fence into our yard ," said Donna. "Our two dogs jumped up and grabbed the cat in mid-air before it even touched the ground. The results were not pretty," Donna grimaced, remembering the episode well.

We were contacted by the same breeder where Doug and Donna obtained their dogs because, I guess, our friends had given our name that we might be looking for a Chow sometime in the near future. He had one 3-month-old female left from the new litter he had just sold off.

"I need to place them with an owner by three months old or they just never seem to adjust and become well mannered animals." The breeder explained that if we would agree to take her, she would be free of charge.

Well, we couldn't resist. Our girls, Jaina and Karen, still in elementary school, were very happy and excited to say the least! We excitedly went to pick her up. The girls immediately decided on the name "CiCi" and it seemed to stick. It was hard to imagine that this lovable puppy could grow up to be a loving, loyal pet, or a mean killer watchdog, depending on how she would be raised. One thing we hadn't really counted on dealing with at the time: We already owned three cats.

"Oh, brother!" our friends just rolled their eyes. "Well, good luck with that!" they snicker.

Unknown to us at the time, our three house cats, Sugar, Tigger and Max, a 6-month-old Manx, were already on the alert for the new intruder. We put the dog inside our fenced yard with her food and water. A few hours later, when we went to check on her, she was no where to be found.

"She must have gotten out somehow!" Karen wailed. "Jaina, let's go try to find her!" The girls searched and searched and inquired of our neighbors. "She must have gotten out through the loose board on the fence," they guessed. All efforts turned up no puppy.

"Karen, someone must have stolen her," Jaina announced sadly to Karen at the end of the day. The girls went to bed with heavy hearts. They only had their puppy for one day and she was already gone, probably forever.

The next afternoon the girls were out skimming the pool. They heard noises coming from under the deck above them. Karen looked up and there was Cici! She had been hiding under the deck!

"There she is, Jaina, look!" It took some coaxing and a little raw hamburger on the end of a stick, but she finally came out. The cats were waiting. Sugar, one of the female Himalayans, hissed and swatted at her immediately. Cici ran the other direction, but Jaina caught her.

"Awwww, poor baby. The cats have been scaring you!" she said, holding her tenderly. "Come on, you are staying in my room, little puppy."

Well, I'm not sure how it all turned out, except over time the cats seemed to train the dog very well, and they developed a very good understanding and respect for each other. Apparently, the hissing, scratching cat was not a creature CiCi was willing to encounter, so she learned what made the cats happy and comfortable and did that. Cici went as far as to let the cats snuggle and hug her and even shared meals with the cats.

Isn't it nice to know that hugging, sharing and peacefulness can also occur among animals? She resisted what her natural instincts urged her to do and chose the path of peace.

I suppose if people could learn the same about their human relationships, it would definitely be a better world.

The Bible says in Romans 12:18,

"Don't quarrel with anyone,
be at peace with everyone,
just as much as possible."

City Cats

by Kelly Wilson Wanamaker

As morning and I take time to reacquaint ourselves, I pull my gray, wooly robe about my shoulders and slide my toes into my worn, soft slippers. My pack consists of my beagle-dachshund-mix, Sarah, and a mom cat with four grown kittens we didn't have the heart to part with. They were alerted by my rising and robe adorning and excitedly piled towards the French doors that let onto the porch of our just-finished country home.

Suburban cats, used to prowling the streets and yards of our left behind neighborhood, eagerly await my rising each morning, peeking at me over covers and around the alarm clock, batting my nose with soft paws, anxious for me to awake and grant them access to explore the new territory of woods and fields and water surrounding our lake home.

Smiling, I open the door and they pile out around me in a mass, running into each other as Curly, my slow, easily confused sweet cat halts on the doormat in indecision and blocks progress. Laughing, I look down at little Sarah, my faithful beagle friend, who feeling the buffet of the crisp December frost, plops her rump down and obviously chooses to stay indoors. I gently close the door behind the last escaping tail and wander into the kitchen for my morning tea, Sarah trailing along happily, the warmth of the heated floors seeping through my slippers.

As the hot water steeps the tea and the warm smell of lavender and mint wafts through my brain, I gradually begin to realize I am hearing the neighbor's rooster crowing in an anxious fashion. Odd, I think, he sounds closer than usual; his constant announcements of threats to his kingdom have become an unwelcome addition to our new life, but, thankfully, are usually a bit muted by the acre of fields between us and his chicken house.

Today, he sounds like he is right under my window instead of a football field away and I marvel at how sound can travel so crisply on cold, winter mornings. Carefully sipping the too hot mug, I wander into the study, Sarah following, and move my computer mouse, bringing the screen to life as I slide into the leather office chair. I hear the rooster again and I stop for a moment, my sleep-fogged brain beginning to process the pieces of information.

Concern nibbles through and picking up my mug, Sarah in tow, I head down the hallway and back to my bedroom. My neighbors, a wonderful, just married couple that bought their home soon after we started construction on ours, have accumulated a flock of rescued chickens and the annoying rooster, each one named and loved, and I would hate to see the devastation on their faces if one of my sweet kitties decided they were simply larger sparrows, of which they were all fond of hunting.

It would not be a good way to start off our relationship with them and as I proceed down the hall, alarm flashes through my brain and hurries my steps. I look out the big picture window as I round the corner and see a flock of brown, feathered, anxious chickens, milling about and clucking on our drainfield directly off the house, certainly not a football field away, the big black rooster puffed up and crowing crazily at the direction of our porch. "Oh no, no wonder they sounded so close," flits through my brain as I yank the French door open preparing to yell to stop the slaughter I could vividly imagine.

Instead of blood and feathers and mangled bird bodies, five pairs of panicked, huge green eyes stare up at me from black and white faces huddled together into one mass of fur on the doormat. As the door opens mom-cat streaks through first, followed by four blurs, each heading straight for the bed and disappearing underneath. Curly comes in last and, even in his bewildered state, catches up, his corkscrew tail catching the bedskirt and billowing it outward with a final pouf before they are gone. Hiding my surprise and amusement, so as not to injure their pride any further, I quickly search the porch and yard for mishaps and, finding none, with Sarah's joyfully barking help, in my slippers and robe, tea mug still in hand, shoo the cackling flock back across the field and home, the rooster crowing defiantly through the process even as he hurries back to the safety of his coop.

Returning to the warmth of my room, I lift the bedskirt and peer under. Five sweet faces look back at me, firmly planted at the farthest corner against the wall, huddled together. No amount of coaxing convinces my suburban cats that the terrifyingly huge, demon-monster birds have gone and it is late in the day before they venture forth and two days before they peek outside to sit on the doormat and watch carefully for them to reappear.

As I recount this story years past, I still smile as I remember the look of shock and panic on their little faces as my city cats reacted to this country calamity, in their minds, birds grown horribly huge and threatening. It also saddens me each day as I open the door in the morning and my little pack slips outside carefully, eyes moving in all directions, looking for danger, even though my neighbors gave up their rescued flock and the annoying rooster long ago, having lost too many battles with the local raccoons.

Gone is the carefree anticipation and rush out into a new and exciting adventure, replaced instead with caution and hesitation, a search for the safe escape and a clear retreat. And thinking about it, I wonder how often in my life I let the roosters of my past take the joy and excitement out of the new adventure that is each day and, instead, spend every moment cautious, wasting precious energy looking for imagined dangers and the quick escape route or safe retreat.

I vow to myself to let my past experiences go so I can step fully into living my purpose, unafraid, trusting that God will protect my back. Jeremiah 17:7-says,

> *"Blessed is the man who trusts in the Lord,*
> *whose confidence is in him. He will be*
> *like a tree planted by the water*
> *that sends out its root by the stream.*
> *It does not fear when heat comes;*
> *it's leaves are always green."*

Coneheads

by Susan Otis

Recentlym my two dogs, Otie and Sophie, had to visit the Vet within two days of each other. They came home with big plastic cones on their heads and had to wear them for a couple weeks. It was such a sad sight.

Poor Sophie was first. As soon as we arrived back home she jumped out of the car with her new head attire and off she ran quickly learning that something wasn't right. She hadn't picked her head up high enough off the ground and got her cone stuck on the drive way. Something had changed; she couldn't navigate the yard, the deck, or the house without bumping into something.

Doing things the way she had always done them didn't work anymore. She couldn't trust her own judgment. She became immobilized, except for following someone right in front of her. Otherwise, she would stand in one place and stare at the wall, the chair, or the porch railing, whimpering. I could be standing right next to her calling her name but with no peripheral vision and an unwillingness to turn her head to the side she was unable to find me.

Then Otie had his little accident and went to the Vet and came home with the same type of cone on his head. Otie's response was a little different. He immediately was immobilized and with head bent downward would stand in one place

BIBLE LESSONS FROM OUR PETS

and stare at the ground. He wouldn't even look up. Actually, it was hilarious.

It took them days to figure out how to manage to get around and function with the cones on their heads. They really never did totally figure it out.

After watching them, I realized that we often respond the same way to pain or loss. We put on our blinders to protect our wound. Our heart equilibrium is off kilter but we pretend that nothing has changed. As long as we look directly in front of us, things appear normal. We do our best to keep up the façade of normalcy.

We keep working, doing, buying, but at the same time we are fumbling around trying to do everything the old way. In reality we aren't looking forward; we are stuck living in the past. We are moving through life looking in our rear view mirror to tell us where to go. Not a good way to drive a car or to live a life. If we don't acknowledge, let go of the loss, and accept that things will never be the same, we can't be healed.

Have you heard the saying "let the past be the past"? I can't say that I thought it very profound, but in reality, it's so true and simple. The past can't be anything but our history, a reference of where we've been and what we've experienced. Today is the beginning of our future.

The Persistent Pup

by Diane Beinschroth

Argh!! Can someone help me?! I have a 106 pound lapdog named Pope. If having numb legs wasn't bad enough, I also can't get anything done when I'm at home. See, my wonderful lapdog is a very persistent dog as well. When I'm at home working on the computer, Pope will just stare at me and will not stop until he gets what he wants. Do you know how distracting it is having a BIG pit-bull staring at you with HUGE puppy eyes? And if you say to me, "Just turn your head," I say, "Posh, you try concentrating on a work project with THOSE eyes burning a hole through you!"

When it becomes apparent that Pope wants something, the only thing left to determine is what that thing is and that is when the real fun begins. I get up from my desk and move to the most likely destination, the food bowl. That's not it?! Ugh… Well, maybe he wants to play? We head to the chew toys. I guess that's not it. Is it possible that he wants to go for a walk? Hmm, let's go outside! After I hunt down Pope's leash, which becomes my leash sometimes, I head outside to take Pope out for a jaunt. But, wait, that's not it? Great! We are already outside, so I might as well wait to see if he needs to use the doggy bathroom. Five minutes later there's

nothing and Pope is still staring at me. Defeated, I head back
inside and take a seat on the couch. The next thing you
know, my little dog in a big dog's body curls up on my lap,
cutting off any blood flow that had once traveled to my legs.
That was it?! That's what he wanted!

Pope taught me a very valuable lesson. He taught me
about persistence and the Bible speaks of that as well. Luke
11:9-10 says,

> *"So I say to you, ask, and it will be*
> *given to you; seek, and you will find;*
> *knock and it will be opened to you.*
> *For everyone who asks receives,*
> *and he who seeks finds, and to him who*
> *knocks it will be opened."*

Think of yourself like Pope — just keep on staring at
God and he will provide. Don't stop. Don't give up. But
unlike me, God knows what you want and won't have to take
you outside only to find out that you really want is to sit on
His lap.

When I found out that all Pope wanted was to sit on my
lap, did I force him to eat his dog food, or to go for a walk?
No! What kind of good owner would I be? This is exactly
how our Heavenly Father is. If we need blessing and are
truly open to receive His blessing, he won't give us poverty.
Jesus continued to say in Luke 11:11-13,

> *"If a son asks for bread from any father*
> *among you, will he give him a stone?*
> *Or if he asks for fish, will he give him*

a serpent instead of a fish?
Or if he asks for an egg, will he offer
a scorpion? If you then, being evil,
know how to give good gifts to
your children, how much more
will your Heavenly Father give
the Holy Spirit to those
who ask Him?"

Our God is a loving and good God. Just like I am a loving dog owner!

The Calm During the Storm

by Joseph Calhoun

Let me introduce you to my hunting dogs — I have two 4-year-old German Shorthaired Pointers named Ruger and Whiskey. They are full of energy and are constantly moving. I recently was married, so their indoor privileges have been more or less revoked and they now sleep outside in their kennel — but that's a whole other story. This story is about a thunderstorm.

One night, I awoke from a very deep sleep at around 1:00 am by the dogs barking. I did what I usually do when they bark and rapped on the window with my knuckles. They are mostly well mannered dogs, so that kept them quiet, for a while. About 20 minutes later, I heard a loud crash on the side of the house, followed by very loud barking. I grabbed my glasses, threw on some shoes and went outside with a flashlight. Right when I opened the door, I saw the lightning flash. I checked the side of the house and some boards had fallen over — no big deal there. All the while, the dogs were barking very loud and very rapidly. I could immediately tell when I got to their kennel that they were scared. The storm had come and they didn't know what to do.

I went in the kennel, closed the door behind me, and sat down by their bed. They were so terrified that they just walked around in circles until I told them to "come." At first I couldn't believe it. I mean, these are my tough hunting dogs! The sound of a shotgun blast is like music to their ears. I thought about it later and realized that for every other thunderstorm that ever came through, they were sleeping inside and I was right there. There was no reason for them to be scared because I was close by. No matter how tough we think we are, it makes no difference when the right kind of storm hits.

Using my calmest voice possible, I sat there for about 5 minutes or so petting them on the head and telling them it was okay. I didn't leave until I could visibly see that they were calm. When they were okay, there was an immediate physical change. I could especially tell it in their eyes. I got them to lay down on their bed and they stayed as I exited the kennel and went back inside. The thunderstorm passed and they didn't bark anymore that night.

As I was lying down, trying to sleep, I was reminded of how similar this situation with the dogs is to our lives when storms come. Sometimes things happen in our lives that we have no control over, just like in a storm. I've had Ruger and Whiskey (who are litter mates) since they were 10 weeks old. Not only can I distinguish one dog's bark from the other, but I can also tell why they are barking — happy, alert, scared. The barks I heard that night were ones I seldom heard before — scared ones. These boys were scared and they needed my help. What I like about dogs is there is no middle ground. They went right from scared to "help me." It got me wondering why we don't do that as humans.

So often, when the storm hits, we over analyze things and try to figure them out on our own. Why isn't "going to God for help" our first thought?

God is always there and ready to help us. He knows our voices and he knows what we need. Just like I could tell that the dogs were scared, God knows exactly what we are going through and has the remedy. It is so easy to get caught up in life that we forget to go to God first. It is strange that when things are going great, God is always on our minds, yet when things go sideways, we tend to forget about Him. The Bible is chock full of verses about how God is always there for us. David wrote about just that in one of the most-memorized passages of scripture:

> *"Even though I walk through the valley*
> *of the shadow of death, I will fear*
> *no evil, for you are with me;*
> *your rod and your staff*
> *they comfort me"*
> (Psalm 23:4, NIV).

Sometimes we need to have the same simple mindset of a dog. In life, when things get rough, we need to go to God first. A simple "help me" is oftentimes all we need. We don't have to conjure up this beautiful, eloquent prayer.

God knows exactly what we need. He is always there to help...and he doesn't have to fumble for his glasses, put on shoes, and grab a flashlight when we come calling.

Garden of Dogs

by Shalona McFarland

We use to have this little dog named Jessie. She was a Pomeranian-poodle mix and she was incredibly smart — sometimes a bit too smart for her own good. We always knew when Jessie had done something wrong because she wouldn't meet us at the door when we got home. Well, one day we came home and there was no Jessie at the door. We knew immediately there was something wrong. As we continued to call, she didn't come at all.

That was quite unusual. When we walked into the house, we saw why she had not come when we called. She just knew she was in huge trouble! She had toilet papered the house! Like, the entire house. I don't know how she did it, but she managed to make about three passes around the middle of the house, fun up the stairs and TP the upstairs as well, without breaking the toilet paper! It was so amazing, we all just laughed.

We walked through the house calling and calling for Jessie. We finally found her upstairs under the bed with her butt sticking out from under the bed. She was sure she was hidden. Of course she wasn't and we knew she was some-where within the house — just like God knew Adam and Eve were still within the garden after they had sinned. He called to them asking where they were and they would not answer. When they finally did answer the Lord, He asked why they had sinned and gone against his word? They didn't know really why, so they blamed it on someone else.

The dog couldn't blame it on someone else, but she certainly could hide from us. I also see the forgiveness of God in this story. Even though she knew she had done wrong and hid from us, when we finally found her, we didn't punish her severely or banish her from the house.

We simply loved on her and laughed in amazement of her accomplishment. I'm sure she thought she was a goner — just as Adam and Eve thought. While they were thrown from the garden, they were not banished from the earth. And while God did punish them severely, He loved them so much He created a royal line of kings that came from those two people that eventually brought forth our savior.

"For God so loved the world
that he gave his only begotten son."
(John 3:16a)

Thank you for being a forgiving Father.

Close Shave

by Nathan Gaub

I've had times in my life where something seemed like a good idea and it turned out to not to be such a bright idea after all. My wife is one of those people who really likes animals. She had three little kittens and those cats love her. I like kittens; the problem with kittens is that they grow up to be cats and cats don't like me. Well, we have one cat that likes me. I kind of like it too; it's a nice little cat, but it started chewing itself all up. It started chewing on its feet and then it started chewing on its back.

Pretty soon it was a ragged looking little cat. And it's a long haired cat. It's one of those cats that are half calico, half afghan, and half dust mop. I don't know what kind it is but it's got real long hair. It just looks like a big fur ball. I took it to the vet and the vet said, "Your cat has a big problem. This long-haired cat is allergic to cat hair."

Now that's a tuff life right there, when you're a long-haired cat and you're allergic to cat hair — there's a problem. But the vet told me, "Don't worry, all you have to do is have the cat shaved down so it's hair is real short and use this medication once a month and everything is going to be okay."

So I called around to some of those animal grooming places to make an appointment. You know, they wanted $100 to shave a cat. I thought, "That's a lot of money!" I don't even think the cat is worth $100, so I figured, "How hard could it be to shave a cat?"

Seemed like a good idea. I went to Walmart and bought a little $12 set of clippers. I thought this is gonna be easy. This little thing will make short work of a cat. Then I got to thinking about it. We live in an RV and it's a really long-haired cat and when I shave this cat we are gonna have enough hair to make another cat. So I need to contain this hair. We have a nice big bathroom there in our rv. I sat down at the only place you can sit in a bathroom. I call the cat. This cat likes me so she comes running and jumps right up in my lap. I'm thinking, "This is gonna be easy." I close the door. So now I have contained the cat.

Problem is I have contained the cat in close proximity to me. I started the clippers. And then I turned off the clippers and got the cat down off the top of the shower, put band aids on all the places I needed them, got the cat calmed down and I started the clippers again. And then I got the cat down off the top of the medicine cabinet and used the band aids that were left. I made a mental note to go to Walmart and get more band aids because I was now out of band aids. By the time I had finished, if you came to me today and said, "I need you to shave my cat," my rate is $400. But it seemed like a good idea when I started.

Well, we're kind of like that with the things of God. We think we've got a good idea, we think it must be godly. But God's plan is not always what seems like a good idea to you and me. We know we need the information, but we don't always listen until we are in a crisis mode. For instance, there are things we can do to put our finances in order so that we don't operate from a crisis mode with God.

The Bible talks about the blessings of God all over the place, but the Bible is full of paradoxes. The bible says things like,

> The first shall be last ... the greatest among us
> are the servants ... if you cling to your life
> you'll lose it but if you give it up
> for Jesus you'll find it.

What makes this last paradox even harder to understand, sometimes, is when we apply it to our finances: "If we hold on to our money, we won't have any."

How does that work? It seems like if I hold on to it, I got it. The Bible says if we really want God to bless our finances, we have to be generous in every way in your life. The more you give away, the more you will have.

Got a Doo-Lemma?

by Brian Hetzer

I can remember about a year ago or so — I was off work for the day and my wife and I were catching up on our "to do" list — work around the house, errands in town, etc. It was early afternoon; we climbed into our car to run some errands in town after finishing the major housework and picking up the "gifts" in the yard that our two lovely doggies always leave us (they are so generous!).

It wasn't too far down the road when I began smelling something in the car that about made me gag! "What in the world is that stench," I remember asking myself. I slowly turned my head toward my wife, giving her the "eye"!! She looked back at me and said, "What? That wasn't me! I thought you did it!" I quickly rolled my window down as I replied, "No babe, that wasn't me... nice try!" It was then that I happened to look down at her shoes and to my horror, I saw a very large chunk of dog crap stuck to the bottom of her right tennis shoe... and she had obviously been walking around on it for awhile, because it was smashed and squirting out the sides of her tennis shoe!!

Way gross and way stinky!! Instantly, almost like in stereo, we both began gasping for fresh air and laughing at the same time! Then, reality hit me — where has she been since walking out in the yard earlier this morning — the porch, the outdoor carpet, inside the house, in our car... oh man, this could be ugly, not to mention a disgusting, smelly mess!

Looking back now, I shake my head and laugh to myself at the humor of that day, but at the same time, it also makes me think about personal offenses and how "stinky" picking them up can be! A personal offense can occur when we take on or engage a real or supposed injustice (someone doing something "wrong" to us or to someone else), which causes strong emotions in us such as bitterness, anger, envy, harshness, cruelty, gossip and rudeness.

Like my wife unknowingly stepping in a hidden pile of dog crap in our yard, we can unknowingly take on an offense, which will quickly begin to leave its trail of anger, bitterness and rudeness wherever we go. And before we realize it, we've tracked it all over the place, leaving ugly "marks" and stinking up the place!

We all have probably known someone who just seems to be bitter and angry all the time. No matter what the situation, they seem to consistently speak out negativity and walk around with a dark cloud over their head. Over time, the result of this offensive behavior is that no one wants to be around them and they unintentionally isolate themselves; which stirs up more feelings of rudeness, envy and harshness. It becomes an ugly merry-go-round. An offense can also be described as a "stumbling block" or "trap." Like that pile of dog crap in my yard... it just sat their, hidden until my wife walked through the yard and unknowingly stepped in it.

It instantly stuck to her shoe and quickly became a noticeable issue wherever she went. However, if she had seen the pile ahead of time, she would have recognized the "trap" and avoided it. And even if she didn't see it initially, but immediately recognized that she had stepped in something, she would have taken care of the problem on her shoe before it began to stink everywhere she went.

The Bible makes it clear that anger in itself is not sin. However, it becomes sin when we choose to hold on to it. It is then that we get caught in the trap of the offense. Ephesians 4:26 says,

> "...don't sin by letting anger
> gain control over you..."

The Message Bible says it this way,

> "Go ahead and be angry. You do well
> to be angry — but don't use your anger
> as fuel for revenge. And don't stay angry.
> Don't go to bed angry."

So, what do we do if we find ourselves having already "stepped in the crap" and we can't get it off our shoes? First, we have to recognize that the problem is rooted in unforgiveness.

When someone has wronged us and we choose not to forgive them (even if we think they don't deserve it), we are making the choice to hold onto the offense and it will never leave us, but instead, continue to grow and grow in our heart like an ugly cancer!

"If you forgive those who sin against you,
your heavenly Father will forgive you.
But if you refuse to forgive others,
your Father will not forgive your sins."
Matthew 5:14-15

When we choose not to forgive another's wrong toward us, God is not able to forgive our wrong toward Him. This opens the door for our hearts to be overtaken and overpowered by the offense, which will produce in us (and out of us through our words and actions) bitterness, anger, rudeness, cruelty, etc. This is a very ugly place to be for us individually and for those in our circle of influence. All of us, at one time or another, will be confronted with an opportunity to be offended. So what do we do when it comes? First, recognize it for what it is and decide up front that you will not take on that offense (yes — that is a pile of dog crap, but I will avoid it at all cost!).

Then, immediately choose to walk in forgiveness and humility. Offering forgiveness upfront is like seeing the dog crap in the yard and deciding to clean it up right then — getting rid of the "hazard" so neither you or anyone else will step in it. In Matthew 18, Jesus describes this situation in this way:

"If another believer sins against you, go privately
and point out the fault. If the other person listens
and confesses it, you have won that person back.
But if you are unsuccessful, take one or two
others with you and go back again, so that
everything you say may be confirmed by

two or three witnesses. If that person still refuses
to listen, take your case to the church. If
the church decides you are right, but the other
person won't accept it, treat that person
as a pagan or a corrupt tax collector."

In simple terms, these are the Biblical steps for confronting someone who has wronged you:

1. Go to them in private. If they confess and repent of the sin, you do not need to share it with anyone else; to do so would be gossip.

2. If he does not repent, go to him with one or two reputable brothers (or sisters) in Christ so they can add Godly counsel to the situation.

3. If he still does not repent, bring it before the elders of the church and let them try to reason with him.

4. If he still does not repent, treat him like an unsaved person. The sin he committed against you now takes a back seat to the bigger issue — the eternal destiny of his soul! He needs to hear the message of salvation and the cross.

Notice that we are to go to the one who offended us first. Often times, however, people try to deal with offenses by airing their hurt feelings out to everyone around them, except the person they should be going too — the one who offended them. When people come to us with a story of injustice, we should always direct them to the one who hurt them and encourage them to work it out. In actuality, by coming to us and not resolving it themselves with the person, they are doing us an injustice.

How? Because we will take on their feelings of offense but have no right to confront their offender ourselves — they have to do it. It leaves us "stewing" over someone else's situation, listening to gossip and can do nothing ourselves to resolve the problem. Not a good place to be!

Yes — offenses are like piles of dog crap and it's always been more healthy for the dogs, my lawn and my family to keep those never ending piles down to a minimum. We want to strive to be people who encourage healing and restoration, not people who enable the growth of "stinky" and "messy" offenses.

The Joy of My Life

by Na Mi Oxford

I have a toy poodle and his name is Joy. He is my shadow and such a joyful little dog. I am so thankful and he is a miracle in my life.

While I was going through physical problems, I realized that I needed something to make me smile and give me laughter. I thought about what that could be ... the answer was I needed a dog, small enough to carry around. Our family has always had dogs, but they were big, hunting dogs. I raised a few puppies, but by the time they were big and mature enough , they became hunting dogs. I needed a dog that was only my dog and a non-shedding dog for allergy problems I had at that time.

A little red colored poodle sounded good to me. I had a poodle when I was growing up in Korea. His name was King and he was a very smart little toy poodle. I wanted a smart toy poodle just like him. But I thought, am I able to take care of a dog? Due to my spine problem, how am I going to carry a dog around? God said, " Yes," then I started searching for a red colored poodle.

One place I went to had red colored ones but there was a lot of in breeding going on and it was just a puppy farm. I didn't want that. I started praying for a red colored poodle and still no luck. After a while, I still was unable to find just the right dog and my search had continued for two years! But in my sprit I saw that little red poodle running around the house and I thought how his color matches our floor.

Even though my search had been fruitless, I continued to thank God for giving me a vision for this particular dog. I kept on believing that God would provide me a red colored poodle and even named him! I wasn't exactly getting the support I needed from some of my family concerning my diligent search. Even my son thought I should settle. "Mom," he said, " I just don't think you are going to find this red colored poodle you want, so why don't you get a white one instead?! " I'll even color it for you," he continued.

So he was obviously as frustrated as I was concerning my hunt, but I was unwilling to settle. But I kept telling Tom, my husband, and Richard that my poodle is out there some-where ... God showed it to me! Still I couldn't find the right one. I just didn't want to wait any longer, so I cried out, "Oh, Jesus, where is my puppy? I don't see it!" Then I happened on an advertisement for an apricot colored puppy. "Hmmm," I thought, "could this be the one?" The ad didn't say that the puppies were poodles, so I decided to take a look. Oh the puppies were so beautiful, how could I resist bringing one of these sweeties home?

They weren't red, but oh so close that I considered taking one home. But my inner voice said, "No, Na Mi, your red poodle is still out there for you." I told the lady that her puppies are so adorable but I want to have a red poodle; it's been over two years now and I am going to keep waiting for my red poodle. The lady also said that she wanted a red colored poodle and if she found one that money was no object. "Great," I thought, "now I have competition!" So after initially becoming a bit excited at the site of the ad, I was quite discouraged. This search had dragged on far longer than I had desired, but I was going to continue to listen to the Holy Spirit and stick to my guns.

A short time after this recent setback, Tom was preparing to go back to work after a long Christmas break. We had decided to go to the store for some post Christmas shopping. Just before we left, I asked Tom to "wait a second," I wanted to take another look online, for dogs, before we took off. When I did, there they were, red colored poodles! And they were only a few hours away in Seattle!!!

So I called the owner and she said there was only one puppy left. She was gracious enough to meet us half way in North Bend. When I saw the puppy, I knew that it was him and I could hardly contain myself! This was exactly the dog that I had envisioned. The feeling of holding this small animal in my arms after a long and emotional search was almost overwhelming.

He was finally with me after over two years of waiting! I named him "King," just like my childhood dog. I started to call him King, but I said immediately, "King" is my Jesus, not my dog's name. How about Joy? Yes, that's right. I need joy in my life again and this puppy is going to bring me joy. Did it matter that the puppy was a little boy? No. I determined that his name was going to be Joy, so Joy it was! He became that joy I needed and now I am growing in healing as he is growing into his doggy body.

Ever since he came into my life he became my prayer partner. He is always on my special prayer blanket with me while I am praying every morning. Not only that, Tom and I started praying together before he went to work two years ago. Of course, he joined us again. While we hold hands together praying, he is on my hand and he drops his head to my hand and lay his head on his paws, and when we say "Amen," he gets up. He knows our prayer is over. His day starts with prayer just like us.

He is such a Joy in our life. I am so thankful to God for his creation. He is my reminder to me of faith, endurance, and patience in Jesus Christ.

> *"My brethren, count it all joy when you fall*
> *into various trials, knowing that*
> *the testing of your faith produces patience.*
> *But let patience have its perfect work,*
> *that you may be perfect and complete,*
> *lacking nothing"*
> — James 1:2-4.

He is now five years old and travels with us everywhere we go.

Loco, the Miracle Dog

by Judy Baugher

The twins Trudy and Judy loved animals, but they especially loved dogs and horses. They spent a great deal of time drawing pictures of horses; they read every horse and every dog book in the school library where they attended. They desperately wanted a dog.

Well, it seemed they were destined to have one. They lived somewhat in the country and walked a mile to school. One day they noticed a reddish fox looking dog on the play ground. They, of course, went right over to get acquainted. The dog seemed to be quite taken with the twins over the other young children that tried to play with him. Much too soon the school bell rang for class.

When school let out for the day, the twins hurried around the school yard looking for the little dog. The dog and the twins spotted each other at the same time and seemed overjoyed to see one another again. The twins played with the dog awhile and realized they had to be heading home. They decided to call the dog "Loco." Trudy and Judy were worried about Loco disappearing before they returned to school the next day so they decided the best thing to do was take Loco home with them!

All the way home they made plans about how to ask mom if they could keep Loco. "Mom, come outside and see what followed us home from school," the twins called out to their mother. Mom was surprised. The twins told their mom all about how Loco was just a tramp dog and really, really needed a home. "Please, please mom," they begged, "Can't we keep him. He is such a good dog and he won't be any trouble. We'll take care of him." Mother was won over by Loco's polite manners and the twins' pleadings.

Loco followed the twins faithfully to school every day. He would play with them during recesses every day and then follow them home. Trudy and Judy worked many hours training Loco. He was a very smart dog and soon learned to perform on command: "Sit," "Shake hands," "Stay," "Lay down," "Guard," "Sit up and beg," "Stand up and dance," and "Speak," that is, in dog language of course. Loco also would be very obedient on a leash.

The school district decided one year the twins were to ride a bus to school. So the first day of school, the twins told Loco goodbye and climbed on the bus and away they went. Loco was quite visibly shaken over not going with the twins. Mother told them that afternoon that Loco sat and watched the bus leave and tilted his head from one side to side as if to think this new situation through. He gave a little cry and took off in the opposite direction. Loco knew a school bus when he saw one; after all he had seen a lot of them. A school bus meant school!!

How surprised Trudy and Judy were when they got to school and climbed off the bus to be excitedly greeted by one very happy Loco. You could not out-smart Loco!! From then on, Loco watched the twins get on the bus, met them at school when they got off the bus, then left school after the last recess, and met the bus at home when they arrived.

One day the twins noticed Loco wasn't his usual bright self and didn't seem very hungry. They told their mom and dad. They decided to keep an eye on him a few days and see what would happen. Loco began to cough and got worse. Even though money was not plentiful, their mom and dad took Loco to visit a veterinarian. The doctor gave them some pills to give Loco, but he said if he was not better after the pills were gone he should be put to sleep. The twins' brother Ron was home on leave from the Navy at this time and there was much excitement as he had been gone for some time in Japan and brought back gifts for his mom, dad, and his three sisters.

The twins faithfully gave Loco his pills, but his health did not improve. When they were in school one day, dad asked Ron if he would take Loco to the vet to be put to sleep.

When this terrible news was given to the twins when they returned from school, they were almost overcome with grief and cried many days over losing their companion of a few years. They talked and talked about Loco for a long time remembering all the fun they had with him and how much they missed him.

Six months later, on Valentine's Day, mother was hanging up the wash on the clothes line when she was startled by a reddish streak that came flying around the side of the house! She could not believe her eyes. It could not be. LOCO!!! He was so excited to see her and barked and jumped up and down. Mother did not know what to think or what to do. All she could say was, "Are you Loco?" She was afraid Loco would leave before the twins got home from school, so she locked him into the screened in porch and watched and waited with him. It was time for the bus to come. Loco began to cry and scratched on the screen door to get out. Mother let him out, and he ran to the bus stop half a block away. But the twins decided to walk home that day and did not get off the bus with the rest of the children. Loco was puzzled and turned his head from side to side and thought. He remembered the twins walked home sometime. He ran back home and sat in the driveway and waited and watched.

Trudy and Judy had just crossed the big highway and were almost home when they stopped and looked and looked. They saw a dog sitting at the driveway. It looked like Loco. But that was impossible — wasn't it? As they got closer the dog barked and ran toward them. It was Loco! The twins were crying by now and so was Loco.

It took weeks to find out what had happened six months earlier to make this miracle happen. A letter finally arrived from their brother Ron in Japan. He wrote that he could not bear the thought of putting the twins' Loco to death and instead had taken him miles away from home and dumped him near a ranch house out in Medicine Valley. Someone loved and looked after Loco and he got well. But in spite of the love these people gave him, Loco could only think of the twins and the love he had for them and began the long trek home. Trudy and Judy loved and enjoyed Loco for a long time. He enriched their lives tremendously.

Even though the twins did not know Jesus, He knew them and heard their cries of grief and returned their beloved pet. Later in life, Judy came to know the Lord and worked in ministry with her husband for many years.

"It shall come to pass that before they call,
I will answer; and while they are
still speaking, I will hear"
— Isaiah 65:24

Carefree Fur Balls

by Karen Henry

I have two small dogs, Ellie and Rhubarb. They are energetic, love to play and love being with family. We got Ellie about 5 years ago at a rescue shelter and Rhuby, this last fall; she was running the streets and no one claimed her, so we did!

It has been a season of change for myself, and my family recently. We are stepping out of what we know to move to a new town with a church plant team. It has meant selling and buying a home, leaving jobs and finding a new job. It's meant our financial situation looks different too.

There have been questions of worry and concern; how will this work, will we find the right place, will we have enough?

As I watch Ellie and Rhuby, running around, doing their doggie stuff. I see they're not worried about anything. Not worried about being fed and having enough, not worried about where they'll sleep or even what's going to happen next. Then I remember, when Jesus is speaking in Matthew 6:25-26:

"Therefore I tell you, do not worry

about your life, what you will eat or drink;
or about your body, what you will wear.
Is not life more than food and the body
more than clothes? Look at the birds
of the air (dogs in your house);
they do not sow or reap or store away
in barns, and yet your heavenly Father
feeds them. Are you not much more
valuable than they?"

Jesus also tells me in verse 33 "…seek first His kingdom and His righteousness, (read my bible, to know Him) and all these things will be given to you as well. 34…do not worry about tomorrow, for tomorrow will worry about itself. Each day has enough trouble of its own."

My dogs know I love them because of what I do for them; they trust me and don't worry.

I know God loves me because of what He's done; He gave His only Son for me so that I can be part of His family and never die, but have everlasting life.

Proverbs 3:5-6 says,

"Trust in the LORD with all your heart;
do not depend on your own understanding.
Seek His will in all you do, and he
will show you which path to take."

Yes, I will continue trusting in the Lord!

Thanks Ellie and Rhuby, for reminding me, I don't need to worry!

On Solid Ground

by Shelly Peterson

It was a quiet morning not unlike any other wintry Saturday in January. We were enjoying the calmness of the day. Morning chores had been done and the ranch was peaceful with a new dusting of snow on the ground. All at once our daughter Amy exclaimed that Sis was down.

This was alarming because Sis was almost 31 years old and getting back up from a lying position had become a feat all of its own. I went to the front window to look with my daughter. I commented that we'd give her a few moments to see if she could get up on her own. After several unsuccessful attempts, Amy decided to go out and encourage her.

Because Sis had shoes on to help her tender feet, she remained unable to get her footing on the blanket of snow that covered the frozen ground. She continued to flip herself over in an attempt to get up; she only tired herself more. As I went to grab a halter and a lead rope, I summoned my husband, Scott, to meet me out front. We tried without success to get Sis on her feet. She could not get her back feet underneath herself and her front feet only slid out from under her.

After several more attempts, I made an urgent call to my brother and sister-in-law. Since they had owned horses for over 20 years, I decided to ask if they had any ideas. Sis had only been down about 45 minutes. They were not too concerned about the length of time and together we decided to try to give her something besides ice to get a grip. We dumped shavings on the area, in an attempt to put something under her that would not slip, but all to no avail. After leaving her to try on her own for about another 20 minutes, we made a call to the vet. He was on another call at the time

and would fit us in as soon as he could.

In the mean time, Sis was already starting to work herself into a lather and was beginning to shiver. I decided to get a blanket to warm her. The problem was by that point she had become frantic and kept rolling herself over onto it. Out of sheer exhaustion, she finally resigned. We comforted her as we waited for the vet, not sure whether this would be the last day we would have our old friend with us.

At one point, as I stroked her head and neck, she rolled her eyes back into her head and her tongue fell out of her mouth. I thought, "We're losing her!" I called to my husband to get our daughter back out with Sis, so she could comfort her. I knew that if this was to be our final moments with Sis, Amy would want to be there, to say her goodbyes. Amy came out immediately, knelt on the icy ground and with tears streaming down her face, started talking to Sis. Sis responded with perked ears and the focus came back to her eyes. We spent the next hour or so crying, praying, and comforting our old friend before the vet arrived.

As the vet pulled into the field, I remarked that it didn't look good. He gave me his usual smile and said, "We're not going to make any negative prognosis till we see what we can do." By that time, Sis had been down over 2½ hours. The first thing he did was sedate her, so he could move her off the ice and begin working on her. We needed to use the tractor to move her to a clear spot in the field. (We had seen plenty of "Animal Rescue" shows, so we were somewhat prepared for what this meant.) When we got her off the ice, we placed her on a canvas drop cloth to get her off the wet ground. Dr Andy wanted to warm her and get some fluids back in her before we attempted to get her up. He requested all the old towels and blankets we could muster to dry and warm Sis. I ran to get these and something to make a rudimentary IV pole.

As I played the role of supply runner, Dr. Andy put my daughter immediately to work, scrubbing the IV site. My husband held Sis quiet, as Amy diligently washed and rinsed Sis's neck, repeating the process several times until the site was as clean as it could be. Dr. Andy then started the IV, pumped up with anesthetics. As the IV was flowing full-bore into Sis, Scott held her down to keep her calm.

When the IV was nearly empty, Dr. Andy started planning his next move. I don't know whether it was the fact that

Sis was warmer or that she had just enough drugs in her to feel better, or maybe a combination of everything, but she seemed to decide that she had in fact had enough. In one swift move, she threw her head up, knocking my husband off balance and pulling the IV out, rolled herself over and bolted to her feet. She was up!

We ran to get a halter on her and a line on her tail, so we could keep her up and stable. We walked her to a stall to keep a close eye on her. Before the next hour passed, she was drying and had stopped shaking. The 24 hours that followed were crucial, but she faired well and it looked like she would be fine.

In the initial days after that memorable Saturday, we had to help her up several times, but almost a year later she is doing well. The LORD has showed us how important she is to our ranch. This event has brought a change in Sis, too. Prior to that Saturday she was getting persnickety and cranky. She no longer seemed to enjoy having her favorite spots rubbed and she would balk at giving me her feet so I could pick them out. But, since that day she has started following us in the field and seeks out our attention. She even lets me pick up her feet with no argument. It's as if she's saying, "I get you guys now, you really love me."

This event continually reminds me of our relationship with the LORD. How many times do we slip and fall and it seems absolutely impossible to get our feet on solid ground? He showed me so clearly how we struggle within our own might to get ourselves back up, but we are completely ineffective. Yet, when we reach the point where we stop resisting the help we need and give all control to the One who knows what He is doing, then we are able to stand on solid ground.

God reassures us in His word and through that reassurance we also can say, "I get it LORD, you really love me!"

> *"In his kindness God called you to share*
> *in his eternal glory by means of*
> *Christ Jesus. So after you have suffered*
> *a little while, he will restore,*
> *support, and strengthen you, and*
> *he will place you on a*
> *firm foundation."*
> — I Peter 5:10

Slither

by Robin Henry

On my 50th birthday I happened to find myself in a pet store. It was the kind of store that took a very "hands on" approach by letting all the customers play with all the animals and many of the adults and children were taking full advantage of that aspect.

There were many kids with their parents in sectioned off places playing with puppies, kittens, rabbits, hamsters, and rats. What really caught my attention was a big, gross python that the store manager was holding. "Eww," I said to myself, "I hate snakes!" In fact, I've hated snakes since I was a little girl. I definitely wasn't going to hang out with the manager!

Then I noticed a little five-year-old boy who was holding a tarantula and he was absolutely mesmerized! As I watched him, I realized he had no fear, but only fascination for this creepy looking creature. His parents told me the only place they could get a tarantula for his son was at this pet store. Of course, I HAD to go to the only pet store in town with all these creepy things around!

"That was it," I thought! If a five year old boy wasn't afraid to hold a big, hairy spider, then I can most certainly hold that slimy python that the manager was holding. I had decided to walk up to the manager and ask him a flurry of questions about the snake. After talking to him for awhile, I FINALLY was able to chalk up the nerve to touch it.

As I placed my hand on its scaley body I realized something: the snake wasn't the cold, slimy beast I thought it was! It was just a beautiful creation of God! Then I took the next step; I asked to hold it! He agreed and passed the snake on to me. It just curled up in my arms and it felt as it belonged there. "Wow," I thought, "not scary at all!" I held onto that snake for 20 minutes and realized I was just like that little boy, fascinated and not afraid.

I will never forget that day, as I overcame a nearly life-time fear of snakes and even bought a snake for myself! It became a reminder to me that sometimes God puts scary stuff in our path to overcome fear and move forward in life.

We have been created not to fear, but to unpack those fears and remember there is nothing to fear because our heavenly Father is ALWAYS with us. Remember what 2 Timothy 1:7 teaches us,

"For the Spirit God gave us does not make us timid, but gives us power, love and self-discipline."

Scaredy Cat

by David Smith

It's another fine afternoon in Yakima, Washington, complete with dimming, cloudless skies. Most of the time in the morning and in the evening, I will stand by at my window and drink a strong cup of coffee as I look out at the beautiful valley that I live in. I can see snow on the hills in the distance and orchards and birds and so many wonderful things. I never tire of looking at nature and taking it all in like a big deep breath.

Many times, my cat Bling is with me. She is a window connoisseur as well! If there is such a thing as reincarnation, I must have been a cat! My cat is an indoor and outdoor cat. We love letting her out to be her wild and ferocious self. She loves to hunt and torture poor little mice and birds and she's very good at it!

On this particular day, Bling looks up at me with her big begging eyes and meows at me as she stands at the door. She wants to go outside, as usual. So I open the door, but she just stands there sniffing the air like she just smells a campfire in the distance or some really good barbeque! I say to her "go on girl, go outside now" in my sweet kitty speaking voice. But she just stands there. She seems very hesitant and yet I know she wants to go out. Why is she just standing there? What is the problem?

I start to get impatient because it is a little chilly and I'm tired of standing there trying to encourage her that it's okay to go outside. She continues to stand there and I give her one last chance to make a run for it. But she decides to stay in. I close the door. This scenario has been repeated on multiple occasions and is definitely not my first rodeo with Bling.

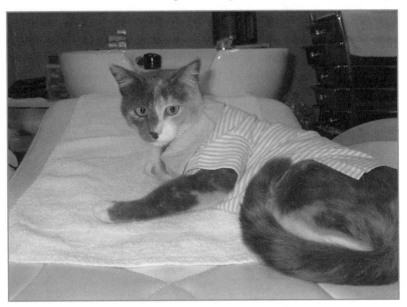

Now, it's too late and she waited too long; instead of going outside she delays and stares. I can tell that she wants to go outside, but is paralyzed. By what? I wish I knew, but I'd like to think it's because she's afraid of the unknown. Maybe there is something out there she's afraid of? There could be a dog, rain, or domineering male cats. Either way, she's being a scaredy cat! So she waits too long, the door is closed and now it's dark outside. It's too late!

73

"How often does this happen to me?" I thought. God opens a door, that opportunity I've been waiting for, and then by the time I decide to go through it, it's too late. Bam!!! The door has been closed — job opportunities, investments, relationships, and career changes, all passed by. Why? Well, in the past, the fear of change, the fear of rejection, the fear of the unknown, and the fear of moving beyond my comfort zone have become road-blocks to potential successes in my life.

Hmmm, I'm sensing a trend! Fear, many times, becomes a paralyzing force in my life, but it doesn't have to be that way. Deuteronomy 31:6 tells us me to:

> *"be strong and of good courage,*
> *do not fear nor be afraid of them;*
> *for the Lord your God, He is the One*
> *who goes with you. He will not*
> *leave nor forsake you."*

Stepping into courage is the antidote to living in fear. I am learning that life is more of an adventure when I take the step and go through the door! For instance, I have been wanting to writing a book in which I could share some of the revelations I have had from watching my cat. I have never been an author, but I have a desire in my heart to be, and feel that God put that desire in my heart.

Who am I to argue with God!? So many times I thought that I couldn't do something like this because I never had the experience or the platform to do so, but the Bible says "with God all things are possible!" What's the worst thing that could happen? I could lose a little money, no one likes it, and

I have a lot of books lying around. That's no reason not to try! It's hard to believe that my cat taught me to get off my behind and do something new regardless of what obstacles lay in my path, but she did; now I think she can learn a few things from me like how to clean her own litter box or get a job and start contributing to her own food bowl!

Maybe Bling really is paralyzed by fear, or maybe she's just a silly cat, but she showed me another lesson (in I Corinthians 1:27) that,

"God uses the foolish things of this world
to confound the wise."

No Duh, Sherlock!

by Joel "Mark" Donahoe

Have you ever wondered why the Creator of the Heavens and the earth and all the mighty angels and all the greatest human beings throughout human history would take such an interest in common, ordinary, flawed nobodies like you and me? That question always used to baffle me until God used a little chicken to help me see how God views His people.

For nearly five months, God used a little Barred Rock rooster to teach me how to experience Him in a way that is far more personal than reading a book (ever notice how difficult it is to have a personal relationship with a book?)!

This particular rooster came to our little farm via the US Mail, along with fifty other little chicks, and looked exactly the same as all of the other little yellow fuzz balls. The weather in Missouri during February and March was way too cold to put the chicks in the drafty hen house, so I put them in my basement with a heat lamp to keep them nice and toasty for the first month until their feathers grew in.

I loved watching the little fuzz balls grow up in the damp, dark basement, which is where I did most of my work. As soon as the chicks grew feathers, the strongest and bravest chicks would jump up onto the edge of the big card-board box I kept them in, and after a brief look around they would jump right back into the box, with the exception of one inquisitive chick.

I couldn't help but notice one little guy would spend hours perched on top of the box just staring at me while I worked. If I made any sounds or sudden moves, he would bob his neck back and forth, or cock his head to the side. I knew I shouldn't name him cause these chickens were going to the slaughter house and, needless to say, it would not be a good idea to get too attached, but I just couldn't help myself. The small chick's inquisitive nature reminded me a lot of the detective, Sherlock Holmes, so that's what named him.

After the chicks had grown feathers, I moved them all out to the chicken coop. I was surprised to find that, unlike the other chicks, Sherlock would follow me around the coop like a puppy and didn't mind me picking him up (most chickens will try to stay away from human contact). He stuck to me like glue and I often HAD to pick him up to keep from stepping on him. He also would make the cutest chirping noises when I picked him up. It wasn't long before I realized that there was no way Sherlock would end up in a frying pain!

For the next five months, Sherlock got the VIP treat-ment; I would take him out of the pen and turn him loose to catch grasshoppers and I also let him eat my wife's tomatoes (when my wife wasn't watching, of course). There were just so many things about the little guy that endeared me to him, but my time with Sherlock would be short lived.

Sherlock was only six months old when he got sick. The local chicken experts thought he ate a really bad bug. I doctored him the best that I could by giving him lots of his favorite food (tomatoes) and plenty of chicken feed with antibiotics in it. For a few days it looks like he was going to make it, but he suddenly took a turn for the worse and died as I was holding him in my arms. Even though I was hardened to death as a 45-year-old man, I shed a few tears as I buried him. I'm not even ashamed to say that I made a promise to him in my last moment with him that when I get to heaven, I will ask my Father if He would bring Sherlock back to me so that I could have him on my little paradise ranch in the sky.

What happened next was a very different experience for me. As I dug that little hole in the ground and placed Sherlock in it, I was flooded with answers to my questions about how he views His people. After years of asking and seeking, God used my little Sherlock to unlock all my questions. The answers came in the form of questions and, to this day, I believe God spoke to me in the simplest way that I could understand. It was a silent and very powerful moment.

If a typical, hardworking, church-going, country boy like you could have a complete change of heart about the worth of a chicken you were planning to eat because he took an interest in what you were doing, and enjoy your attention and company, isn't it possible that your Creator would enjoy your attempts to know Him better?!?!?! Isn't this how this little rooster that was destined to reach the frying pan managed to get to you? Don't you think your Creator would enjoy all of your questions, or you asking Me for advice, or just telling Me what's bugging you? Imagine how much I could teach you if you really enjoyed hanging around Me more than listening to the radio, or watching TV? When are you going to stop doubting My goodness and start trusting that I gave everybody My #1 rule because I truly WANT to be known and loved? It is because I truly want you known Me that I wrote My book, the Bible, so you can see it all in black and white and remember My instructions so that you can have the blessed life I want from you? What else do I have to do to convince you of My love for you? I demonstrated how much I love you through Jesus, My only begotten Son, so what else do I have to do to convince you that I truly have your best interest at heart?

Ever since God used that little rooster to convince me of His desire to be found and known by those who "diligently seek Him," I never struggle anymore about getting to know Him in a more personal way. Just remember, when you are wondering if God really wants to know us small fries that He created us in His likeness and sent His son to die for our sins to get even closer to us. It's not about what we have done, rather it's all about His love for us. A love that is beyond our comprehension. So let's put down our TV remotes to spend a little more time with Him.

And all of this I learned from a curious rooster named Sherlock......

Sugar's Daddy

by David Smith

My dad is the most wonderful man I have ever known; he is caring, strong, supportive, an animal lover, and just about the biggest teddy bear there is. So when my dad was diagnosed with a severe case of prostate cancer in the summer of 2009, I was devastated. What?! This man who was always so strong and whom I couldn't imagine not in my life was now suddenly going to be in the fight of his life and I would have to come to grips with the fact that my time with him was winding down like a countdown timer that spelled impending doom. My father was now faced with his own mortality.

My parents were very aggressive, by searching alternative remedies along with traditional methods of handling cancer, but in this time, they also sought "the Healer." They received Godly council, attended faith and healing services, and pursued the Lord unlike any time before. During this challenging time, my father had his wife and all of his children to strengthen and encourage him, but he also had someone a little smaller in stature beside him this entire time. Sugar, a brichon-maltese mix, would steadfastly walk beside him during this trial. Through thick and thin, good news and bad news, that little white fuzz-ball would stick closer to my dad than velcro. Sugar loved my dad, especially the treats that he gave her, but in reality, she just loved being with him. She really just wanted to be with him any chance she got, and would sleep on him nearly 24-7 if she could. Sugar brought joy to my dad with her upbeat personality, her sweet face, which almost always appears to have a smile on it, her insistence for people food, and her running outbursts that always ended up with her jumping into my dad's lap.

When my dad's health deteriorated further, it became even more difficult to separate him and Sugar. She also began to mope around like she knew he wasn't doing so well. Sugar was a part of our family and seemingly felt the pain of seeing our father in his condition as his own kids did.

On April the 26th of 2011, the Lord took my father's pain away and he left us for a better place, but he left us wonderful memories, a loving family, and a great amount of valuable life lessons. One of these lessons involves his relationship with Sugar and that true friendship is very valuable. Proverbs 18:24 echoes this sentiment,

"A man of many companions may come to ruin, but there is a friend who sticks closer than a brother."

And while Sugar was just a dog, she remained very close, regardless of what challenges life brought. I know I can use friends like that. How about you?

Snug as a Pig in a Rug

by Howard Gunnherson

When I was a child, I had several "pets." I lived on a farm in Minnesota, so sometimes any animal became a short term pet. My father raised a lot of pigs, which were all raised to be bacon on someone's plate, but one I became a lot more attached to than others. His name was Henry, a red Duroc pig.

He needed a lot of help when he was born, as he was sick and he would not have made it if it weren't for some late night bottle feedings. It was at that moment that I became

My Tippy

more attached to this pig over the others. I named this pig Henry. By the way, it's always a mistake to name an animal that will eventually end up on someone's plate. I was still prepared for his eventual demise as my father constantly warned me to not become too attached and that he would be "sent to market" with the other animals when he was big enough. But we really enjoyed his fun personality while he was with us.

He wasn't very cuddly with people, being a very independent animal, but he took a liking to my dog, Tippy, and vice versa. One of Henry's funnier quirks was when he was still on the smaller side, he would wait just outside the kitchen door and when someone would open the wooden screen, he would quickly sneak in. Once in human territory, he would roll all of the throw rugs around the house with his wet snout! Eventually, we would find Henry asleep in one of those rugs.

We all thought that was very funny. He got so comfortable inside those rugs that he would be out like a light. Who could blame him? Those rugs were dark, soft, and really warm, which would knock anyone out cold.

How does comfort relate to our faith? Well, if we get too cozy in life and faith, we can get lazy and basically fall into a

spiritual coma. As Christians, it's important that we are always alert and focused. When life becomes too comfortable, with no further growth, or no spiritual challenge is when we are in danger of a comfort coma. Comfort can rob us of our strength and dependence on our Father. While we may never want to go through earthly trials, they can be used by God to refine us in our faith. James 1:2-4 says for us to:

> *"Consider it all joy, my brethren,*
> *when you encounter various trials,*
> *knowing that the testing of your faith*
> *produces endurance. And let endurance*
> *have its perfect result, that you may be*
> *perfect and complete, lacking in nothing."*

We don't have to go seeking for difficulty, but when a giant pops up to stop us from where we know we need to go, let's not snivel in front of that giant, that challenge, but stand tall and firm. Grab that sling shot, or that ability God has given you, and put that beast down. Live your life to the fullest. Make challenge an exciting adventure, not something to fear and hold you back. When Goliath, the mammoth giant, appeared, do you know what David did? He didn't run, but stood his ground and then struck down his enemy! God wants us to do the same.

What has comfort and the giant robbed you of? Is it that thing that you love to do? It's time to take back what the enemy has robbed you of.

Our First Family Dog

by Beth Gatrell

One August day in 1997, we picked up this cute little black puppy. It was very exciting since we had just bought our first house and had no children yet. I thought we would play every day and this dog would love me forever! Well, he seemed to have a different idea of love and play in mind. He would run like crazy when I'd take him for a walk and occasionally even made me fall. Then he'd always seem to have accidents when I was the only one home to clean them up.

Still, I loved this puppy and thought as soon as he gets bigger he'll understand and become a lot nicer. So he grew and grew to a monstrous sized Black Lab and decided his favorite thing to do would be to hover over me as I was awakening in the morning and growl.

This is when I realized that we had a special relationship … he was going to push the limits just like a child and when he didn't like something he was going to let me know. As long as we did it his way, the world would revolve on a happy dog-like axis.

And we had lots of fun going on trips and boating and just loving our dog. Then one day we had a child of our own and the dog was no longer the only attention stealer. We were worried that he might not like the idea, but love took over and he would sit in front of the baby and keep watch over her. Anyone that wanted to see that baby had to first be approved of by the dog. The dog would play with the baby who grew to be a little girl and becaome a big sister and the Black Lab loved them both.

But after 15 wonderful years as the first child, the dog's bones got weak and his body got old. On Friday, February 4th, 2011, we made one of the hardest decisions our hearts have ever had to make. Blacker had to be put to sleep. With his "human family" by his side, we watched him take his last breath and cried, not for him, but for us. What that dog had given us was true love and we were going to miss it!

Rest in peace old buddy!
Love, Beth Gatrell & Family

Bad Dogs

by Mallory Huibregtse

My husband and I have two Yokipoo dogs named Bentley and Gunther. We never thought we would have dogs, let alone inside dogs. But we have quickly become "dog lovers" and can't imagine our lives without our two rugrats. They have taught us a lot about ourselves and also about God. When we leave our house, the boys stay in the kitchen and it doesn't matter if we are gone for 5 mins. or 10 hours, every time we walk through the door it's as if it's the first time they have seen us in years.

The unconditional love, passion, happiness and excitement they have when they see us is just the same as the very first time. They are jumping up and down on us and wanting to lick (kiss) us all over. They welcome us with open arms and hearts..

That's exactly how God is, if we ever fall away from God, or decide to "leave" him, it doesn't matter if we haven't talked to Him for 2 days or 15 years, he still welcomes us with unconditional love, passion and authentic excitement every time we decide to walk through His door again and come home to Him. He doesn't treat us any differently no matter how long or short we have walked away from Him.

Just like Bentley and Gunther, it doesn't matter how long we have left them at home or how short a time, they are still always there just as excited and happy to see us. It doesn't matter if they got in trouble by us when we left or if they get in trouble by us when we get home, they still have the same unconditional love and excitement for us.

It's just like the story about the prodigal son in Luke 15:11-32: the son left his father's home and sinned against him, but when he came back home, his father welcomed him with open arms and even had a celebration for his return. The father didn't care about what his son had done to him in the past or how long he had been gone from home; all he cared about was that his son was home and he used to be lost, but now he was found.

Remember that God always loves you no matter what. You can run to Him at anytime and He will always be there for you to love and accept you!

The Squirrel and the Truck

by Susan Otis

While out on an early morning walk I watched a squirrel as it labored to carry a pine cone much larger than its body up the road. It weaved back and forth from one side to the other reminding me of the old Laurel and Hardy movie of a man trying to carry a refrigerator up a flight of stairs by himself. The cone was so large that the squirrel was unable to see where it was going.

As I turned off the road onto my drive way I heard a logging truck speeding down the hill. I wondered if the squirrel had the presence of mind to drop the pine cone and run for its life or whether that internal drive to store up for winter would be his ruin. Immediately, I thought, "There is a lesson in what I just witnessed."

How often do we lose sight of life and all that it can be because something internal that we don't understand drives us to prove to ourselves or someone else that we are "good enough" or that we deserve to be happy and loved? We keep trying to achieve, prove that we are worthy, and work harder to validate our existence, or earn enough to buy what we think looks like success, in an attempt to quiet the voice that makes us doubt we are "good enough." Instead of the pine cone, we are carrying a burden that blocks us from seeing a clear view of what God has to offer us. We become a slave to this internal quest just like the squirrel is to storing for the winter.

I don't know about you, but after months of unsuccessfully doing life a certain way, I finally got tired of it not working for me. I had been carrying a load that I wasn't meant to carry. 1 Peter 5:7 says

> *"Cast all your cares on him*
> *because he cares for you."*

That means our worries, needs, heart issues, the things we care about, people we love, and our hopes and desires. Can we trust that he cares more than we do about the most important issues of our lives?

That little squirrel will forever remind me of why I shouldn't be carrying burdens that are not meant for me to carry.

The Stray Cat that Never Left

by Tyler Keefe

When I was a child, my mother liked to feed the stray cats around the house. I didn't quite appreciate this as I feared my friends would start calling her, "The Crazy Cat Lady." That being said, there was one cat that caught my eye. He was a grey scraggly looking cat, one that was very skinny, but always seemed to have energy. Most days I would pet him and just let him hang around me, but there were some days that I wanted nothing to do with him. When he'd come up to me for attention, I shoved him away or simply went inside and ignored him. There were many times that I felt bad about this and wished I hadn't done it, but it was just a stray cat to me.

One day he stopped coming around. I didn't think much of this at the time, but then one day turned to two, then to five and so on. I assumed he died or got picked up, but I was never quite sure and I know I will never know what really happened.

Now, many years later, I look back and wonder what happened or how this can apply to my life. I think, "Why was I so mean to the cat; he just wanted attention." It didn't take me long for my spirit to quicken within me what had bothered me. I sometimes think about God in the same way as that scraggly cat. Not that he looks sickly, for God is the maker of the heavens and the earth and is the creator and foundation of strength. But I feel that if I do not give the Lord the attention I know he rightfully deserves that he might leave me. I know God doesn't need my attention, but he wants it. Often I am too "busy" to give him my time or efforts. And that fear that one day he will leave my side and will not come back around grips my thoughts.

But then I think, wait a minute, doesn't God say,

"I will never leave you, nor forsake you,"

so that we may boldly say,

"The Lord is my helper ... I will not
fear what man shall do to me?"

He told us this and I have no reason to not believe him, because he doesn't change his mind as wind changes directions like most people do. He is the same yesterday, today, and forever.

And with a solid rock, like God,

"whom there is no variation or
shifting shadow ..."

I know that we will always be there for me as he was there for the prodigal son. I take solace and am comforted by those thoughts. Praise God for his steadfastness, who is right next to me, unlike that stray cat......

Tweety, God's Special Bird

by Judy Baugher

"Mom, mom!" I heard my daughter Paula shout one spring day. She came into the house holding a very tiny baby bird. The bird was all pink stomach and mouth and not much else. Not even a feather! The two of us went outside to see if we could find a nest that the baby could have fallen out of, but to no avail. Paula found the baby bird on the wooden walk way located between the house and a storage building located a few feet at a higher ground level. The ground was bare except for pine needles. There was absolutely no place that the baby bird could have come from!

I knew that for the baby, whom we had now named Tweety, to live he had to have small grit to digest his food. We quickly found some old parakeet grit and put a few pieces of dry dog food to soak in hot water. We were thrilled when Tweety seemed to thrive on his diet of the dog food, pieces of greens, and insects Paula hunted for him. We would dip the wet dog food pieces into the grits once or twice a day to add a few bits to it.

Feeding a baby bird is no small task as they awake at dawn screaming for something to eat. Paula was very dedicated and stayed with her task of being Tweety's mother.

Tweety soon begin getting feathers. When he had all his feathers he didn't need a cover at night any longer. As soon as he could see, Paula became "mom" to him. He loved her and knew her voice instantly and would call out to her when he heard her.

Tweety soon became quite a fun part of our family. He loved attention, especially to have his head scratched. He would fly to us and land on our shoulder and hop down our arm to one of our fingers where he would ruffle up his feathers and bend his head down begging to have his head scratched. We would call him to come when we had caught a fly in the house. We would hold the fly between our fingers and hold out our hand for him to land on and call out, "Tweety come here." My, did he love flies!

When he was full grown, Paula began taking him outside to really fly. He loved to be out in the wilderness on top of the mountain where we lived. Paula could leave Tweety out all day and go out in the evening and call him, hold out her hand, and he would fly to her and land on her hand ready to go home to his cage bedroom inside the house.

When we would go to camp meetings, Tweety loved to ride on Paula's shoulder all about the camping area while she rode her bike. When we went to workers' meetings at the church camp, there was Tweety in all his glory entertaining everyone. He loved to go to the children's meeting outdoors with Paula and would hop all about visiting all the young people as they sat about on the ground. We were concerned that he would get hurt by landing on someone's head or shoulder that did not know him and they would hit him, but I guess word got around about "that bird Tweety." Everyone loved Tweety.

Interestingly, no one could ever tell us what kind of bird he was. We all pulled out our bird books, but poor Tweety never matched up with any of the birds in it. Tweety gave our family, especially Paula, a lot of joy.

"Are not two little sparrows sold for a penny?
And yet not one of them will fall to the ground
without your Father's leave (consent) and
notice. Fear ye not therefore, ye are of
more value than many sparrows."
— Matthew 10: 29, 31

If God cared so much for Tweety that He brought him to our family to save his life, don't you think He can take care of you?

V is for Victory!

by Buffy Smith

I went from being a drug addict who even spent some time being homeless to a born again-crazy-for-Jesus Christian who was determined to do my life different. I chose to go to beauty school. Between school and work I was at church learning about Jesus and learning the Bible. As soon as I graduated, I got a job at a salon in the mall.

After only a few months at my first job as a stylist, I began to have shooting pains in my right arm. The pain would shoot from my elbow to my pinky and ring finger every time I lifted my arm higher then my waste. Unable to work, I quit my job. My doctor had me start physical therapy. For the next few years my body seemed to be warring against me. I had many different physical problems and I was told there were some structural problems in my body which was the cause.

This was a very discouraging time in my life. But I was determined to stand on God's word (Philippians 4:13) that says,

"I can do all things through Christ
who strengthens me."

96

I stood on the word of God and went back to doing hair and was very successful although I had pain much of the time. During this time my parents had a couple of cats. These cats were outdoor cats and I loved them and looked forward to spending time with them. There were a few stray cats that would come into our yard and eat the cat food. We would try to shoo them away so they didn't eat it all.

We started to notice a white female cat around our yard. She was a really mean cat. Not friendly at all. But she was pregnant and we let her stay in the yard. I love kittens and was fine with taking responsibility for them. As soon as the mean cat had her kittens, I went looking for them. What I found was like nothing I had ever seen.

One of these kittens had back legs that were completely straight! I wasn't sure, but it looked like her joints were backwards. Her back legs were more like human legs. Her hip was normal but the knee joint and the next one down above the ankle were backwards. Her ankle joint was normal. Her legs naturally were straight up by her face and they were open as in a V shape. I must admit, the first time I saw her, I felt a little sick to my stomach and I thought "poor kitty"!

She seemed healthy enough although she was deformed. I took her in to show my parents and I don't really remember what they said but I think we all agreed that this must've been the result of inbreeding. I took her immediately to the vet. I wondered if they had ever seen such a thing. I really wish I had a picture because she was so unusual looking. The vet did not seem too disturbed by the joints and quickly came up with a solution. She said that because the ankle joint was correct, the cat could possibly learn to walk but she would need a lot of physical therapy! I was excited because I had been through physical therapy quite a bit and I had such a respect for how well it works. If I had never had all these problems I never would've known how to help this cat.

The vet taped that cat's legs together at the joints so her hips would align and her legs would not go straight up by her head and open in that V shape. So now she looked more like if you were sitting on the floor with both legs straight out in front of you and your face down with your nose touching your knees. She had tape on each little joint. What a sight to see!

I took her home and explained to my parents the situation. She would need me to stretch her legs back and forth to strengthen her hip joint and eventually help her to walk somehow. I determined to help her live as good of a cat life as possible. I had seen videos of dogs with no back legs before. Sometimes the dog had a thing with wheels attached to the back half so they could walk around freely. But cats don't just walk, they jump, they climb, they hide behind things. I was determined to help her walk.

I had learned from Proverbs 18:21 that

"Death and life are in the power of the tongue, and those who love it will eat its fruit ..."

so I named her "Victory." We called her Vicky for short. It was summer as she grew and she was very healthy. I stretched her legs for her twice a day and as she got bigger I would set her in the grass and play with her. She had no idea she was deformed! She began to move around all by herself and I could see she wanted to walk.

Luckily the grass had not been mowed and it was just high enough to hold her up because she was so small. I realized this was the thing we needed. That grass was enough to hold her up as she made her first steps. Her back legs were still taped so they were basically one leg. I spent a lot of time having her follow me around the yard with that tall grass holding her up. Soon I was able to take off the tape at her joints and she didn't need the tall grass to hold her up.

She never did walk normal. The back legs were always kind of a pair. She moved more like a bunny rabbit. When she stood her butt would stick up so high in the air with her back legs straight as can be! We couldn't believe she could walk across thin boards as graceful as any other cat. If she had fallen from up high she would've landed on her feet. She could run and she could jump. She lived up to her name and was victorious. She was not born physically like any other cat but it did not stop her from living and doing all the things other cats do. I don't know if she had any pain but people were always amazed when they saw what she could do as deformed as she was.

We all are born with weaknesses and we all go through struggles. I learned from this cat that I don't have to let my limitations stop me from living the best life I can. I can ignore them and just live and do what I can. God's word tells us a lot of things that seem to be opposite of what we think and a scripture that I think illustrates my story and Victory's story is 2 Corinthians 12:9 that says,

"My grace is sufficient for you, for my power is made perfect in weakness."

99

What my D-O-G Taught Me About G-O-D

by John Molinario

December... Night...Cold... and my fluffy 4-1/2 pound friend was not home. A combination of my panic and how sacred my black Maltese-Yorkie (I call him a Morkie!) must have been just overwhelming. I wondered how he felt being all alone after getting out of what I thought was a securely fenced-in backyard.

My adjoining neighbor called me earlier that day at work asking if Meeko could spend the day at her house. When he was done visiting we told her to simply put him over the fence and he would come in through the doggie door ...which this time the family had forgotten to put in place before leaving for the weekend. Not being able to enter the house with no one home, Meeko apparently "freaked" and pulled a Houdini, miraculously escaping out of the yard in a search for his family (to this day I do not know how he did it!). Neighbors saw him out on the street and tried catching him, knowing no one was home. He ran away from everyone.

As I arrived home, I was greeted by my distraught neighbor who had Meeko earlier. That led to a man-hunt (or should I say dog-hunt) for my little pal. We frantically grabbed flashlights and took to the yards, streets, and open-space walkways where we would take him for walks thinking those would be familiar territories for the terrier! At 1AM I was the only one remaining in the search party that had dropped off one-by-one as there was nothing more they could do.

I could not sleep knowing, he was out there, scared, cold, alone... LOST. If not freezing to death, I had visions of him being a meal for an owl or coyote. Even his orneriness would not save him from such creatures. I could only hope someone picked him up and would see a flyer tomorrow.

At sunrise, I began the process of placing flyers on mailboxes and cars saying to myself, "He's gone, or at least walking around scared." All of a sudden a voice as clear as friends chatting over coffee said, "Stop right now what you are doing, John. Drive on the parkway. You will find him there." It stopped me dead in my tracks. I remember pausing, cocking my head aside saying to myself, "Huh?" It was a scary and surreal feeling hitting me like an invisible hammer square in the face. But what was even more scary was the "voice" was right! A quarter mile away, I found my buddy walking confused down the sidewalk along the parkway! I could not believe it. Spooky.

What had happened here? I feel God wanted to show me He DOES exist and DOES watch us. I surely thought Meeko was, at best, going to start a new life with a new family and, at worst, be "a goner"! As a result of God's intervention, we are celebrating Meeko's 15th birthday at this writing and he is as loving (and cantankerous) as ever!

This was Divine intervention. How has God shown Himself to you, especially in troubling times even when you are too focused on the task at hand? Do you forget He is there watching on the sidelines? I did. This was an amazing experience. But was it really a surprise? After all, it was GOD doing His thing, talking and revealing Himself in His time. I found out He does not always show up when WE ask.

But what is important is that we learn He is there, whether we feel His presence or not. I guess this was designed as an airy faith-builder. As the cliché goes, God works in mysterious ways... even through a pet.

1 Kings 19:12 tells us,

> *"Then He said, 'Go out, and stand on the mountain before the Lord.' And behold, the Lord passed by, and a great and strong wind tore into the mountains and broke the rocks in pieces before the Lord, but the Lord was not in the wind; and after the wind an earthquake, but the Lord was not in the earthquake; and after the earthquake a fire, but the Lord was not in the fire; and after the fire a still small voice."*

It was in something as simple as a whisper that God's presence was in, not the fire, strong wind, or earthquake. God could have chosen to speak to me in any way, but he used His voice to speak to me and used a dog to teach me something new.

Molly or Bling, Israel or Palestine

by Shelly Smith

Hi! I am Shelly and Molly is my baby, she is a cat. Like many people, my cats are my babies; I love them, spoil them, scold them — but most of all I LOVE THEM!!! For the 1st three years of Molly's life she lived peacefully (although Abby, her big sister would beg to differ) with myself and her adopted older sister. Life was happy and peaceful and other than having to share the house with Abby, Molly could roam the house freely, without fear or a need to be cautious.

Then one day, a little dog named Sugar came to live with us. Although Sugar is not Molly's favorite housemate, her intrusion into Molly's life was minor in comparison to what was soon to come. My parents had built a large house and we (Molly, Abby, Sugar and I) were all moving in to that house, too. Originally, it was just this small group, but soon there would be an addition to our happy little group — my baby brother David, his wife Buffy and their cat Bling.

Molly and Bling are like oil and water — THEY DON'T MIX. There are moments of peace, but they are short lived. Many times I hear fights going on upstairs or down the hall; frequently you will hear me yelling "BLING SMITH!!!! BEHAVE!!!!" (This gives David and Buffy quite the chuckle.)

Bling likes to find herself hiding places where she will lie in wait for Molly to come by — and then the fur flies!!!

Now Bling is not a total monster, don't get me wrong, she has moments of sweetness and snuggles and I do love Bling, but Molly and Abby are MY CHILDREN. This little cat relationship has given me a glimpse of how God feels about Israel and any person/nation who opposes Israel. There are times when I yell at Bling, "I swear if I get a hold of you I'm going to kick you into next week"!!!, but my soft animal heart would never allow that — maybe a spanking. My sentiments are paltry in comparison to how God feels and yet He continues to extend grace and patience towards those who would destroy Israel because of His great love and desire that all his creation be reunited to Himself.

On a side note, as I was typing this little tale, I was thinking about all the times I take Sugar walking and occasionally there is a dog who might be threatening. I observe and assess the possible danger, grab Sugar up and hold her close until I feel the danger is gone — how many times has God done that for us without our knowing it? How great is our God!!!!!!

Loyalty

by Michael Martel

*"He who pursues righteousness and loyalty
finds life, righteousness and honor."*
— Proverbs 21:21 NASB

My dog Haley is almost twelve years old. For a Bernese Mountain Dog that is a very old age. Most Bernese live to seven or eight. Ten is old for them. Big dogs suffer from all sorts of maladies — joint, hip and other arthritic problems. A lot fall to cancer. Haley has suffered from each. She has had two knee operations, each of which cost the price of a nice used car. She has had several tumors removed and the veterinarian charged a nice price for the operation. Many times people asked me if I was crazy spending that much money on a dog. They told me they would have put her down.

Haley might not run around like she once did. She acts pretty stiff in the morning when she starts moving around. She seems to be a bit hard of hearing. Sometimes she doesn't bark when the door bell rings. She, however, is the same loving, trusting loyal friend that she has ever been. Finding the means to make her healthy was the right thing to do.

Loyalty is not something to take for granted. During the course of Haley sharing her life with us, I have been seriously sick three times. Once was with food poisoning, another was with whooping cough, and the other was a bad bout with the flu. Each time I spent about three days in bed. Haley lay at the foot of the bed on the floor the entire time except for food and business breaks. She was the most loyal friend I could ask for. Each night when we get ready for bed, she makes the round to see if each one of us are in bed and only then will she take her place at the foot of the bed.

What if, at Haley's first knee operation when she was six years old, we had put her down? We would have missed half of her life and her time with us. Each day she greets me coming in the door with the same wild enthusiasm. No matter how hard my day has been, Haley always brings a smile to my face.

Finally, what kind of example would I have shown to my son as for loyalty and Christian charity to have our family pet put down because of cost? Following the Word in action provides an example to our children for them to follow. It is often true that the example one sets for their children is the example the children follow in treating their own parents. Right actions and loyalty will be repaid by those that observe these actions.

Haley might not make it around the block much anymore and she is a little slower getting to the food bowl. At the same time, she is as she ever was, a true friend.

Last Cat Standing

by David Smith

Carpet, painting, and hammering, oh my! The summer of 2007 was a whirlwind of construction and remodeling, in preparation to sell our first home. Not only were we knee deep packing and basically turning our little home upside down, but we were both as busy as can be with our jobs. On top of all of the normal moving craziness, we had to prepare moving our family, all five furry felines. Their names were Kaiser, Boots, Socks, Bling, and Shorty. Buffy and I loved our family very much. Shorty was inherited from Buffy when we married, Bling was found by Buffy, hurt and abandoned in a parking lot, and the rest were kittens that Bling had six months after we found her.

These cats became replacements for the children that we didn't have. We loved every one of them and their unique personalities. Shorty was the poster child for why cats shouldn't be inbred; he had goopy eyes, ulcers in his mouth, and a bad sinus problem. He was also one of the most smothering, loving cats I've ever known. Even to the point of being the stalker cat of the group. At times, I would wake up to find him staring at me. Kind of creepy......

Boots was kind of a cry baby, who would just follow us, complaining. Why was he so upset? I don't know, perhaps he wasn't upset at all, but I sure like to think he was. He would just cry until either one of us would let him in, but at least he toldus what he wanted, in the most persistent way possible.

The little sweetie was Socks. She was definitely the runt of the litter and was really fun to dress up in cat cloths, as she would just go limp, like a pouting child. She was also the only cat that I could hold like a baby, and actually liked it! I loved to hold her up to the side of my head and listen to her purr like a roaring motor boat.

My buddy was Kaiser, who was a grey beast, and dominated the rest of the cats. Chasing his mom became his favorite game, and he also loved to sprawl out, completely stretched, just about anywhere. I say he was my buddy because he loved to just chill out with me while I was playing video games. Did he want me to pet him? Not necessarily, he just liked to be next to me, and I loved it!

The mother of all these kittens was Bling. She is a no nonsense cat, who for being a rescue, sure has a strong sense of entitlement. We were there to please her, not the other way around. We really got a chuckle watching her running around with a belly full of kittens; she was this scrawny looking cat with this HUGE gut wobbling back and forth! Shortly after the kittens were born, we got to see her mothering instincts, which were beyond cute. The very first place she hid the kittens was behind the warm tv, and let's just say that became tiresome since that spot was the official litter box for awhile. Then she would hide them in a dresser drawer. Sure, we could have closed the drawer to prevent that from happening, but the cuteness factor was off the charts, so we didn't mind too much, as long as there were not poopies on our cloths. Bling would take the kittens back and forth between these two locations several times. I would have had a little bit more variety. Why not behind or on the sofa? Or under the bed? But I am not a cat!

At the time of our moving, this was our large family, and now it was time to start moving them to their new home. Our plan was to build a cat house to hold them in, so as to get them used to being outside in a new place and not bolt, never to be found again. But our plans were thwarted by a series of disheartening events. The first event happened on a rainy evening before we were going to begin moving the cats. I remember drinking a cup of coffee while reading my Bible in our temporary new home, and received a call from a friend, "David, Socks is dead."

"What," I thought, "Was he mistaken?" I was hoping beyond all hope that he was wrong. Socks had become my favorite cat at the time, and strangely enough, I was hoping he was talking about Boots. I loved Boots, who looked very similar, both black and white, but I didn't have the same connection with him as I did Socks. Once I heard this shocking

news, I raced to the house we were selling to see that underneath a tree in the back yard was indeed, Socks. From what we gathered, she was ambushed by a dog. I immediately grieved the loss of my baby girl, and buried her under that tree, which she loved.

With our recent loss, Buffy and I decided not to hesitate in taking the remainder of our family to the cat house. We gathered them all up, besides Kaiser, who was hiding somewhere, and took them to their new home; a ten by ten wooden shelter with a mesh door. First went Bling, then Shorty, and finally Boots. What I didn't notice, and Boots did, was a weak spot on the door. He shot through that weak spot like a speeding bullet and wouldn't stop. He was gone and wouldn't answer our pleading. Only the next few days we could hear his distinct cries from the distance, but there was no way he was going to come to our calls. We were fortunate enough to get the door shored up enough to where we could contain Shorty and Bling. But both were very frightened being in a new and unfamiliar environment.

With our family of five down to three, we immediately went to gather Kaiser, who we assumed would be ready to come out of hiding by the late afternoon. Sure enough, he was there, and we were both relieved to have our big gray cat corralled in the car. We arrived at the "cat house" to deliver Kaiser to his mother, and my wife held on tightly because he was a very powerful cat. While approaching the door, a pair of big dogs from next door rushed to our position, and while there was a fence separating us from them, Kaiser didn't know that and quickly overpowered Buffy's death like grip. This normally very loving cat, became quite insane at the sound of two big dogs, and the flight or fight instinct took over. And now he was gone. Buffy and I were shocked. In the span of two days we had just lost three family members. There was a lot of second guessing that still happens, and knowing that we could have done things differently to ensure our families' safety still haunts us.

Fortunately, we had two children left, and to make sure they were used to their surroundings, we kept them locked up for just over two weeks. We then released them and had them follow us around to make themselves feel comfortable. And they did! Shorty and Bling were very grateful to be released from their prison and would follow us very closely. Buffy and I were very happy to have Bling and Shorty after the dramatic events of the last few weeks.

The next morning we went out to greet our remaining cats only to find one cat left, Shorty. In a panic, we walked through the orchards, and the grounds of the property to find nothing. Our temporary joy of having both Shorty and Bling diminished with our family whittled down so dramatically. Well, at least we had Shorty. For a few weeks, he would love Buffy and me with his usual viciousness as we visited them at the unfinished house in the middle of the

orchard. We were overjoyed that his quirky personality remained at the house, and would pester those working on the house by rubbing aggressively against their legs. Then one morning even Shorty disappeared and was alarmed greatly by reports of him limping the afternoon before we came to check on him. We seemingly walked miles to find him, but Shorty was nowhere in sight.

Now our family consisted of just us, my wife and me. And the prospects of moving into a beautiful house were diminished without being able to share the large property with all our cats. We continually prayed the ones who ran away would come back or were found by good people. One evening two months later, Buffy and I began loading our belongings into the nearly finished house, and out of the blue I heard a desperate "MEEOOWW," and a shadowy figure coming at us out of the darkness. It was Bling! I had thought she was gone, picked off by coyotes by now. Our reunion was with great emotion, and I could even tell Bling was ecstatic to see us!

Through all of the purring, petting, tears, and laughter, I felt the comforting hand of my Father. I felt sad about losing all our cats, and here was the last furry face I expected to see! Having my Blinger back was the kind of the gift that, at the time, I needed most. James 1:17 says that

> *"Every good and perfect gift is from above,*
> *coming down from the Father of the*
> *heavenly lights, who does not*
> *change like shifting shadows,"*

and Bling's return is still one of the greatest gifts God has given me besides salvation and my amazingly beautiful wife. She is a gift because God has used her to teach me many things and is the inspiration for this book. I still think about how she survived for over a month without us. Did she eat cat food from neighboring cat's bowls, or did she survive off mice? But in the scheme of things, God kept her safe for me, and that's all that matters.

Ricardo's Bunch

by Richard Yoccom

When my wife and I met, we had no idea what we where getting into. We where blending a family, not of just human children but animal children as well. I had one boy and she had two girls. That didn't seem too bad, but that's not taking in consideration that we also had an animal kingdom living in each of our homes. My wife had two cats and a dog and I also added two cats and a dog. So the number of critters, and yes, I consider our children critters, that I became responsible for doubled to a grand total of 9. Yikes! lets just say that life became hectic!

The dog my wife brought to our newly shared home was a chocolate lab named Reese. He was older and was missing a couple of teeth, and he was trained but definitely not apartment material; one wrong move and you were in for a big surprise! One thing I noticed was that Reese had really bad gas and believe me he was rank; you couldn't blame his gas on anyone else. I am not exactly sure what death smells like, but I bet that his gas was pretty close to it. Another funny quirk was when my wife and kids would come home and the garbage would be strung from every end of the apartment.

It was amazing at the mess he would make! He caused my wife and kids a lot of grief but looking past the nastiness, he was a great dog and super faithful. My faithful companion's name is Checo. He is a Cheepoo, which is an ugly, but cute long and course haired, wiry dog who  seems to have the whole bathroom thing backwards. Checo seems to think that when you let him in its time to go to the bathroom. I still don't get it and, as a guy who would like to keep things clean, this habit really drives me nuts. I really used to hate him but rather than try to figure him out with doggy psychology, we have made him an outside dog. Now I love him!

And now for the cats, first there's Taco Sauce. Taco Sauce is young and frisky, you know one of those cats that sees something out of the corner of her eye, runs and pounces at the speed of light. Absolutely a true terror in the night. When we moved, we had to transport her to my house, so we put her in a box, held tightly with duck tape, making it nearly impossible for a trained professional to escape... she did. Keeping her contained was like trying to contain a Tasmanian devil.

Then there's Sunshine. I have never seen anything like Sunshine. She has these crazy eyes that totally give her personality away. She is schizophrenic; you can actually see the paranoia in her eyes in how she peeks around corners and just freaks out on every sound. When we meshed families you couldn't find her. She hid for days, even weeks.

Chelsea is our fat cat that would never get enough exercise. We would always find her asleep in the cupboards — the linen cupboards, the kitchen cupboards, or whatever cupboard she could get into. Also, I kinda think she has sleep apnea. I don't know if you know what that is, but if you ever heard your older grandfather snore, that is what it sounded like sometimes, but amplified by a factor of 10. I would sometimes find myself getting frustrated and would have to wake her up because it was so loud I couldn't hear myself think.

And last but not least is Callie. Callie is our beautiful calico cat. She doesn't have any special powers but is very vocal as she just talks and talks and talk and talks. She will just sit at the door and meow for 15 minutes straight, rubbing the door down to nothing until one of us lets her in. And she is a very loving animal, even to the point where she will buff the hair off your legs if you let her go back and forth, rubbing and purring like a little motor boat with fur.

Well, those are my animals' personalities. Since we combined our households together, we have reduced it down to three: Chelsey died, bless her heart, Reese's poop  was just too big for our yard and now he has a wonderful home on a lake, and Taco Sauce has a great home in Ellensburg, and the rest of them were kicked outside with plenty of heat, food, and water.

We loved all their personalities, even though they could be overwhelming within one household. When my wife and I married, we fully accepted each other, our children, and our pets. And I'm grateful to have a God and church that fully accepts me and all my personality quirks. It's like my household, but 500 times bigger! All those people living lives in unity with one purpose, loving Jesus. Sure, things can get interesting with arguments and being irritated at that guy who picks his nose during church, but I wouldn't have it any other way. They are my family and we're God's family. We not only love God, but by his command, we love each other,

> *You shall love the Lord your God with all your heart and with all your soul and with all your mind. This is the great and first commandment. And the second is like it: You shall love your neighbor as yourself. On these two commandments depend all the Law and the Prophets."*
> (Matthew 22:37-40)

117

The Case of the Missing Leash

by Brian Dollerman

When I was a kid, I bought a puppy—a little white and orange Brittney Spaniel. I named her "Gretchen."

Brittney Spaniels are bird dogs. They are bred to hunt. I wasn't a hunter, but she was. She loved to run. She "pointed" when birds flew by. She chased any animal that was smaller than her. She dug into mole hills, caught and ate moles (truly disgusting to watch).

Gretchen tried to tolerate the leash but she loved to be free. I would often find her running around chasing various wildlife in the horse pasture behind our house.

Jesus Christ purchased our freedom. He has given us a new nature: one that loves to walk in freedom. John 8:36 says,

> *"So if the Son sets you free,*
> *you are truly free."*

2 Corinthians 3:17 reminds us,

> *"Wherever the Spirit of the Lord is,*
> *there is freedom."*

We have a new nature — one that has been recreated in the likeness of Jesus Christ. This new nature is free — free from condemnation, free from the past, free from destructive habits that chain and contain us, free to be joyful, free to live and enjoy this life that God has given us!

We have been unleashed. In other words, if you are a Christian, it's your nature to be free just like it was Gretchen's nature to chase birds. Unfortunately, we sometimes get chained up, hindered, or put back on a leash. We allow hurts, regrets, old habits, fears, insecurities, greed, selfishness, and other negative forces to attach like a choke-collar around our necks.

I remember a time when we couldn't find Gretchen's six-foot long leather leash. It was a rather expensive leash — one that the dog obedience school had recommended. Everyone in my family got blamed for misplacing it. No one confessed and it was still missing.

A few days later, evidence appeared—proving that Gretchen was the culprit in the case of the missing leash. She had eaten it. The leash didn't digest well… so there were many little chunks of leather in Gretchen's dog piles around our lawn. Gretchen showed us what she thought of the leash we used to hold her back. She chewed it up and expelled it. She left it in piles around the yard.

Jesus paid a high price for our freedom. We are meant to be free. Don't go digging through piles of poo looking for a leash that has already been destroyed.

"So Christ has truly set us free. Now make sure that you stay free, and don't get tied up again…"
(Galatians 5.1 NLT)

Tiger, the Repeat Offender

by Ghyrn Wakefield

We have a little orange and cream Pomeranian named Tiger. He is four years old and yet still thinks he's a puppy. He is the baby of the family, and always wants to be the center of attention. He has no qualms about hopping up on the couch and walking across the laptop computer keyboard or stepping all over the book in our hands. He is an incessant licker and when we pull him away from our faces, his tongue keeps licking the air.

Tiger has a couple of weaknesses. He simply cannot resist dirty socks and dirty Kleenexes. If anyone of us leaves their socks on the floor, Tiger finds it, quietly sneaks up on it and tiptoes out of the room. We often find him lying on his side, just leisurely nibbling on a dirty sock.

Tiger loves to steal used Kleenexes from one of the little waste baskets in the bathrooms and go rip it to shreds, leaving little piles of shredded tissue on the floor. If Tiger is notably quiet or absent, we can often follow the trail of tissue to find him lying on his belly, eyes to the floor, and ears way back with a guilty look on his face.

The funny thing is, we have scolded him many times, shaking our finger at the crime scene evidence and delivering a very stern, "No, no Tiger!" The guilty look on his face reveals that he knows he shouldn't have touched the forbidden items, and yet time and time again he steals Kleenexes and dirty socks. Even though it's irritating to clean up his little messes or scoop up the slobbery socks, we still love him. We vow to not leave our socks lying around and keep the wastebaskets emptied, but still some things get past us.

This reminds me of how much God loves me. Time and time again I mess up, and each time God forgives and helps me move on. Romans 7.15 NLT says,

> *"I don't really understand myself,*
> *for I want to do what is right,*
> *but I don't do it. Instead,*
> *I do what I hate."*

Verse 24 continues,

> *"Who will free me from this life that is*
> *dominated by sin and death?"*

Thank God! The answer is in Jesus Christ our Lord."

The Rescue

by Ruth Gunnarson

Heidi was a little black poodle who thought she was a people. When we got her, she was about 3 years old, and cooped up at the Dumb Friends League (what we called this particular Humane Society) in Denver. We were told that she didn't do well with children, and we later deduced that this was because she had been abused — probably by a man because it took her quite awhile to warm up to Howard.

When we got her, we had just moved to Denver, both of our boys had left home and I was so lonely that I needed something to keep me company. I knew I wanted a breed that didn't shed and went looking for a smaller dog like a poodle or a mix. She happened to be a purebred. They actually had a "visiting room" where we spent some time together to see if we would "bond" before they let me adopt her. When I saw her, I loved her and she just cuddled as close to me as she could — all the way home.

From that day on, she was "My Dog." She followed me everywhere like a shadow — always wanted me in her sight. She looked at me with those big black eyes, and I knew that no one else loved me so unconditionally. She wouldn't relax and just lay down in my lap until she had spent some time just looking into my eyes. In time, she warmed up to Howard, but mostly, she was my baby. A few weeks after we had gotten her, I went on a Woman's Retreat and was gone for a couple nights. Howard said she wouldn't eat the entire time I was gone. She just moped around until I came home. She did the same thing the few times we had to "kennel" her because we were going out of town and couldn't take her with us.

Any time we were gone, it was like she had springs in her legs as she would jump in the air to welcome us home. She would jump up into my arms and nothing made her happier than to have us home again. When I took her to be groomed, she knew how pretty she was and acted like she was a princess. She never was very comfortable with little kids around. When little ones were after her, she would come and hide by my legs until I asked her if she wanted to go to her bed. She would run for her kennel and knew she was safe when she was in it and the door was securely latched. Every night she was ready to go to her bed. All we had to say was, "Do you want a treat, Heidi?" She knew it was bed time and was happy until morning.

Heidi loved us — and we loved her — for about 12 years. She moved with us to Yakima in 1997, and she was our faithful companion for several years until a lot of her hair turned gray and she yelped when we went to pick her up because her body was giving out on her. The possibility that she probably had

123

something seriously wrong with her was becoming a reality. I remember the day we took her to the vet and talked about our options at that point. He told us she probably was not going to get any better and that she was in constant pain plus she was losing her bodily functions which made her as frustrated as it did us. We said "good-bye" to her that day and the last thing I remember was how she looked into my eyes with love and let us know that she was glad she came to live with us. We buried her in a special place on our hillside. I lined it with rose petals and knew that part of me was buried with her. As I Corinthians 13 says,

> *"Love is patient, love is kind. It does not envy,*
> *it does not boast, it is not proud. It is not rude,*
> *it is not self-seeking, it is not easily angered,*
> *it keeps no record of wrongs. Love does not delight*
> *in evil but rejoices with the truth. It always*
> *protects, always trusts, always hopes, always*
> *perseveres. Love never fails. But where there*
> *are prophecies, they will cease; where*
> *there are tongues, they will be stilled;*
> *where there is knowledge,*
> *it will pass away."*

I still think about her and the joy she brought into our lives. I don't think I ever want to own another dog, but I am so glad I had the opportunity to have this one own me. Maybe some day we will meet again — over there where we both will be young again. And while some may think I rescued her, but at a time when I was very lonely, she rescued me.

Blue

by Jason Holt

I have a miniature schnauzer named Blue. He loves to play fetch, unlike any other dog I have ever seen. He will bring a ball to you and wait patiently, expecting you to throw it just so he can bring it back and do it all over again and again and again.

One day when it was over 101 degrees, I decided to see how long he would continue to bring the ball back. I stood in the shade and threw the ball at least 30 minutes. On the final throw, he chased down the ball and sat down in the shade. Victory I thought. Nope, he sat for 30 seconds and then ran the ball back over to me for some more.

This dog is relentless. It reminds me of how God relentlessly pursues us so that we can have a relationship with Him. God sent Jesus Christ, His only son, to earth to die for our selfish sins so that we can have a relationship with him. He did this knowing full well that most would choose to reject him.

Romans 5:8 says,

"But God demonstrates His own love toward us,
in that while we were still sinners,
Christ died for us."

Just like my dog's refusal to stop playing fetch, God refuses to give up on us by giving us every possible chance to have fellowship with Him. We were created to know Him and be known by Him.

Besides an obsession with playing fetch, there is one other thing my dog loves to do — be with me. He is always happy to see me. There have been times when I have forgotten to feed Blue or let him go to the bathroom or just ignored him, but no matter what I do, he always wants to hang out with me. It's comforting to know that Christ is the same way, even though I don't always give Him my best, is always ready to hang out and continue our relationship.

Romans 8:38 says,

"For I am persuaded that neither death nor life, nor angels not principalities nor powers, nor things present nor things to come, nor height nor depth, nor any other created thing, shall be able to separate us from the love of God which is in Christ Jesus our Lord."

126

A Steer Named Wicked

by Ken Trainer

I was raised on a ranch and at the age of twelve I had saved enough money to purchase my first steer. Wicked was a range steer, meaning his life was going and doing whatever he wanted. At the auction, when we went back to load him into the truck, we knew we had a live one after he chose to bust thru the 2 x 10 board fence instead of going thru the open gates. We finally had to rope him and use the rope to control his direction and even with the ropes, he managed to run head on into the side of a truck.

When we finally got him home that evening, I had made up my mind that he was one WICKED steer and that would be his name. Wicked lived the remainder of his life out on green grass pastures with fresh water and feed each day.

He really didn't have a care in the world, but he always seemed to make the wrong choices. I remember coming home from school one day and found that he had crashed his way thru the chicken coop wall. I don't know why he went into the chicken coop, nor did I ever discover why he decided to burst through the other side rather than going back out of the hole he had already created.

I reflect back on my life and how much I am like Wicked. I have made choices in my life that caused damage and destruction with no regard to how it would affect those around me. God has placed an open door in front of each of us, but we will do everything in our power to make our own way and do our own thing (the fences).

God placed guides in my life to lead me, my parents, grandparents and teachers, but I choose to fight against them just like Wicked fought the ropes. When I finally did accept Christ as my Lord and Savior, I still, at times, do the things I don't want to do and rebel against God (the chicken coop). I thank God for His Love for me, because unlike Wicked, I have a Savior who loves me no matter what I have done or will do. He is willing to forgive me when I make the poor choices.

Here are a few verses that reflect making right spiritual and life choices. Mathew 7:13-14 says,

> *"Enter by the narrow gate. For the gate is wide*
> *and the way is easy that leads to destruction,*
> *and those who enter by it are many. For the gate*
> *is narrow and the way is hard that leads to life,*
> *and those who find it are few."*

Proverbs 14:12 says,

> *"There is a way that seems right to a man,*
> *but its end is the way to death."*

But unlike Wicked, we have a shot at changing our ways and making decisions that aren't hard and lead to a lot of bumps and bruises.

Dan, the Church-Going Beagle

by Ken Gray

Imagine my excitement as an eight-year-old boy when I discovered I was getting a dog. My cousins were moving away and the day we went to say goodbye, there was a stray dog hanging around in need of a home and me in need of a dog. I named him Dan because my cousin's name was Dan and Daniel Boone was my favorite TV character. So Dan and I became the best of buds for the next twelve years.

One lesson my parents were teaching me by example was the importance of church attendance. We were there every Sunday morning and evening without fail. Those were important days and years in my life; they not only established the habit of regular church attendance, but it was a time of spiritual growth that still keeps me spiritually strong today. But it wasn't just my parents that were teaching me about church attendance. The Bible (Heb 10:23-25 MSG) tells us,

> *"Let's see how inventive we can be in encouraging love and helping out, not avoiding worshiping together as some do but spurring each other on, especially as we see the big day approaching."*

Because we lived near the church, Dan was also a regular attendee. His attendance encouraged everyone; when you arrived at church, Dan was there to greet you and when you left he was there wagging his tail, saying goodbye.

Our little country church had no air conditioning so on hot summer days we opened the windows and doors to keep it cool. But when the door was open, guess who would appear through the door and come walking up the center aisle of the church? You guessed it, Dan.

My dog would always end up on the very front pew, encouraging all of us to be committed to gathering together. Heck, if a dog can do it, anyone can, right? Dan was always there, I don't think he ever missed a service.

We can all take a lesson from Dan, encouraging everyone to be the best church attendee they can be — not to attend church for attendance sake, but to serve, worship, and love as one.

Little Foot, the Box Turtle

by Ken Gray

Some friends gave our kids a Box Turtle named Little Foot. Little Foot lived in an aquarium, but we often felt sorry for Little Foot because her world was so small and would let her out to roam around the house. One day Little Foot was missing!

We searched and searched the house, but no Little Foot. We finally decided she must have gone out the door sometime and escaped to the vast world outside. It was October in the state of Washington and cold weather was on its way. Finally, in January, while searching through some boxes we had stored in a back room, we were shocked by the site of a turtle tucked in a box. It was Little Foot.

As I reached in to pick her up, I expected her to be long gone, but she was alive! She had spent the last four months in hibernation. We brought her out near the fireplace and as she began to warm she came out of her shell and began to crawl about.

Sometimes when things aren't going well in life we retreat into our shell. The Bible tells us to:

"Stoop down and reach out to those who are oppressed.
Share their burdens, and so complete Christ's law."
(Galatians 6:2 MSG)

When things are hard, share them with your friends; they can lift you up in prayer and help lift your burden. We are to be their for each other, as Christians, and pick them up, just like we picked up that sleepy turtle from a box.

The Visitor

by Susan Volonino

Bailey, my Shih Tzu/Pomeranian cross dog knows where we're going as I put on his special collar and leash. He's raring to go and I know that there will be smiles, stories and some tears along the way.

As we approach the building, he's straining on his leash, wanting to go inside. There might be some treats left on the floor for him! First, we have to wipe his paws and make sure he looks nice. I buzz the door, enter and see the seniors in the large room. Some are patiently waiting for lunch at their tables, others are watching TV and still others sleep in their chairs oblivious to the sounds around them.

We go down one corridor of the Seniors Home and as soon as we turn the corner, I hear "Poodle" in a German accent coming from the elderly lady in the wheelchair. "Oma" is delighted to see Bailey and on more than one occasion has taken him for a ride on her lap. She's pretty active for a 99 year old! Bailey patiently lets her pet his head with both hands stroking his ears a little too roughly for his liking. I'm not sure if she understands English but I chat away to her about how soft he is and how he likes to visit her. After a few minutes of enjoyment for her, me and, hopefully,

Bailey, I ease him off her lap and let her know we will be back another time to visit.

Many seniors have Alzheimer's and I'm never sure how much of our visit is getting thru to them. Often Bailey just sits on their lap and I put their hand on his fur hoping that maybe they will connect with him. "John" sees Bailey and can only laugh at him and says "look at his tongue" as he sees Bailey's pink tongue against his tan and cream fur. At least he is enjoying our visit a little bit.

Often in the seniors home, the residents are enjoying a nap at the same time we are there visiting. We check all the rooms though just in case one of them would enjoy a visit from a small fluffy dog. Bailey lies on their beds with them even though his tongue starts to hang out and I know he'd rather be on the cool floor. I've heard some of the same stories over and over again but we listen as they talk and pet the head of the animal in their memories. I know that we may be their only visitor that day or for some that week. Some of their smiles have not been seen for quite some time and the nurses are amazed what miracles my dog can elicit from them.

Our visit time finished, we head out, promising to come again. Paws must be wiped and his regular collar put back on. Depending on the season, once outside he looks for the nearest bush or rubs his face in the snow. He's happy to be outside but I know the next time I ask if he'd like to go visiting, he'll be more than willing to go.

We all have giftings and abilities to offer other people. Bailey isn't involved in politics, nor is she active in the fight for poverty, but she plays her part. She makes these elderly individuals happy and she exploits her gift to the fullest.

What is your gift? Who has God designed you to be on the earth? Have you found that yet or have you let that go to serve only yourself? Some are leaders, some are scientists, some are handymen, and some are servants. Some make people laugh and some people can help others morn. Many expect God to solve every problem like He's a cosmic vending machine, but Got has given us the abilities and powers to make this world better. This is not for our glory, but His. 2 Corinthians 4:7 says,

"But we have this treasure in jars of clay
to show that this all-surpassing power is
from God and not from us."

The treasure is us, it's that precious gift inside of us. Let's let our talents shine for us, for others, and for God.

Letting Go Is Never Easy

by David Alexieff

I read a quote once that read, "When the time comes to let go, some people sense and accept it; others find it more traumatic. Letting go can turn the time ahead into a new opportunity!" — Anonymous

When my wife and I were first married, we did what most young couples do. We got a pet! Neither of us like dogs so much and birds are a little noisy. Fish are a chore and she said "No" to a snake. So we agreed on a cat. My motto had always been, "Will swerve to hit cats!" I know that's not the best motto in the world, but I just don't like cats!

Anyway, back to the cat. We got our cat from a friend of my cousin who found our cat in the barn by itself. It turns out that the mother cat had given birth to her kittens in a field nearby and was trying to get her kittens to the barn. Tragically, the mother cat was found dead with a kitten in her mouth as she was run over by a tractor.

My wife picked up the kitten and she drove her home. When my wife arrived home, she shared with me that she had held the kitten in her hand all the way home. Right then the kitten's name came to me, "Toonces!" I remember watching older Saturday Night Live skits with Toonces the driving cat and thought it would be a great name.

Toonces was a black and white cat with a little white near her mouth that made it look like she was smirking all the time. We grew to love her like she was our own child. We bought her special things, including food, toys, scratching posts, catnip, kitty bling (collar with jewels) and more. We even bought her Christmas presents! She had her own spot on our bed where she slept every night.

Throughout the years we had a couple moves to different homes and each time we would pack Toonces and her belongings and move her with us. It would take a few days for her to adjust to each new home, but when she did she made it her own.

When our daughter was born, we worried about how Toonces would respond. She responded with love! She slept at the foot of our daughter's bassinet at night and throughout the day. And she would hang out whereever our daughter was during the day! Really cute and surprising.

This brings me to the letting go part. We made another move and when we signed our lease we were told that we could not have pets. So, we had a choice to make. Lie and keep Toonces or find her a new home. We chose to "let go." It was a hard decision to make yet it was the right decision for our family. The family that took Toonces is an amazing family that loves all animals. And they welcomed her in with open arms.

After 11 years of loving a cat like a child, my wife and I let go. We know without a doubt it was the right thing to do. With a new baby, we needed to focus our love and attention on her. Toonces was a huge part of our lives and still has a special place in my heart. There are millions of cats in the world, but there will never be another Toonces the Cat!

There are all sorts of things that we, me included, can let go so that we can move forward. But in letting go, we can always have faith that God will provide. Sure, we let go of Toonces, but in return we gained a family and a home.

"Let us hold unswervingly to the hope we profess,
for he who promised is faithful"
(Hebrews 10:23).

The Day the Monkeys Got Drunk

by Larry Malcom

In the 1960's, we were missionaries in the Congo living in the Ituri Rain Forest. We had four children and four pets: a dog, a cat, and two monkeys. When the children were outside, the monkeys ran free. They would ride on the kids' shoulders or on the handlebars of their bikes. They played with everything the children played with.

At night, each monkey was on a leash in its own tree in the yard. This kept them from wandering off and kept them safe. They had been raised from an infant by people and couldn't fend for themselves. Each morning and evening they were fed a meal of rice cooked in palm oil along with fresh fruit.

One time when we were gone for three days we put out water, fruit and plenty of cooked rice for them. When we came home we found them staggering around like they were drunk. They couldn't climb their tree and it was just comical to watch them. I asked the watchman if anyone had feed them the native beer. He gave me an emphatic and brief, "No!"

Later on in the day, one of the workers at the Bible School came by, observed the monkeys, and told me they are drunk. "Really," I thought, "it's kind of obvious!" He then asked what we fed them.

I answered, "Cooked rice and fruit." So then he asked how long the rice had been in their dishes. When we told him it was sitting out for three days he informed us that the rice and fruit had actually fermented in the tropical heat. So our monkeys had themselves their own private brewery!

If only our exotic pets would have heeded the advice of Ephesians 5:18, which says,

> *"Don't be drunk with wine, because that will ruin your life. Instead, be filled with the Holy Spirit."*

But no, they had to fill themselves with something other than what God had intended instead of His amazing presence. From that time on we put a stop to the monkey's heathen ways. But for that day we had two intoxicated primates.

Lessons from Tucker

by Brian Fitzgerald

Tucker, the Labrador that trained me for over ten years, passed away this past February. Over the past decade, in my educational process, Tucker taught me many things about life.

In my efforts to immortalize our wonderful dog, I thought I would share a few "Tuckerisms."

1. Life is short, play hard — always!

2. We are all going to die someday; who knows, maybe you will exit this planet doing something you love.

3. We serve a magical and mystical and merciful God.

4. Always be thankful for the life we have been given.

5. Every life is sacred! Every person, animal, every dog, duck, deer, elk, pheasant, goose. Have honor and respect in every passing of their life.

6. Tucker taught me that there is no second chance in suicide.

7. The love of your dog has no measure.

8. God is all about Love and Forgiveness. He is always graceful and He always has perfect timing.

9. Respect life; it will be over in an instant.

10. Love, love everyone the way dogs love, happy, joyful and full out 100%!

11. Tucker taught me you cannot control anything but who you choose to spend time with; make wise choices.

12. Today, Tucker taught me about true character. The character of love, honor and respect in what friendship means. He also taught me that some people don't live by that same code.

13. Tucker was a true hero and a teacher today. He taught a group of young hunters the meaning of life and how important it is to have gun safety at all times.

14. Tucker taught me that some people do not have compassion or respect and that we are not allowed to judge other people.

15. When you climb into the "foxhole of life," choose your partners carefully.

16. Be kind always and be grateful.

17. Look for the lessons in every moment and every circumstance. He is always teaching us in every moment, both the good and the bad.

18. Pain is the action of growth. In the pain is where all growth happens, don't run from the pain.

19. Be a good steward; take care of everything God has entrusted to you.

20. In a crisis a Man's true character will always be exposed.

21. Nurture your true friendships.

22. God's Mercy is amazing.

23. God is good!

Thank you Tucker, for making the last decade with you so enjoyable. Your zest for life and the joy you had for every moment was a pleasure to be around. I will never forget the cold and frost covered mornings that we shared together chasing ducks and geese and pheasants.

I loved watching you work and all the energy you brought to the game. My fondest memory will always be you carrying your steel dog dish around with you to tell me it was diner time. May God Bless you and keep you at His feet.

Your Hunting Partner,
Brian

www.biblelessonsfromourpets.com